# 6TH GRADE
# at HOME

## A STUDENT AND PARENT GUIDE
### with Lessons and Activities to Support 6th Grade Learning

The Staff of The Princeton Review

PrincetonReview.com

Penguin
Random
House

The Princeton Review
110 East 42nd Street, 7th Floor
New York, NY 10017

Published in the United States by Penguin Random
House LLC, New York, and in Canada by Random House
of Canada, a division of Penguin Random House Ltd.,
Toronto.

ISBN: 978-0-593-45033-8
eBook ISBN: 978-0-593-45035-2
ISSN: 2766-2373

The Princeton Review is not affiliated with Princeton
University.

Editor: Selena Coppock
Production Editors: Sarah Litt and Lyssa Mandel
Production Artist: Deborah Weber

Printed in the United States of America.

10  9  8  7  6  5  4  3  2  1

First Edition

The Editor would like to thank the Content Developer for
*5th Grade at Home* and *6th Grade at Home,* Mr. Patrick
Brady, for his hard work on these two titles. He jumped
into the project with tons of ideas, expertise, and
imagination, and never stopped helping out and
contributing throughout the workflow.

**Editorial**
Rob Franek, Editor-in-Chief
David Soto, Director of Content Development
Stephen Koch, Student Survey Manager
Deborah Weber, Director of Production
Gabriel Berlin, Production Design Manager
Selena Coppock, Director of Editorial
Aaron Riccio, Senior Editor
Meave Shelton, Senior Editor
Chris Chimera, Editor
Anna Goodlett, Editor
Eleanor Green, Editor
Orion McBean, Editor
Patricia Murphy, Editorial Assistant

**Random House Publishing Team**
Tom Russell, VP, Publisher
Alison Stoltzfus, Publishing Director
Ellen Reed, Production Manager
Amanda Yee, Associate Managing Editor
Suzanne Lee, Designer

For customer service, please contact
**editorialsupport@review.com**,
and be sure to include:

- full title of the book

- ISBN

- page number

# CONTENTS

# Introduction

## You and Your Child

Your job is to help your child excel in school. Everyone agrees that children bloom when their parents, family, friends, and neighbors nudge them to learn—from the Department of Education to the Parent Teacher Association, from research organizations known as "educational laboratories" to the local newspaper, from the National Endowment for the Arts to kids' shows on TV.

But state standards hardly make for enjoyable leisure reading, and plowing through reports on the best ways to teach math and reading can leave you rubbing your temples. You're caught in the middle: you want to help your child, but it's not always easy to know how.

That's where *6th Grade at Home* comes in. We identified the core skills that sixth graders need to know. Then, we put them together along with some helpful tips for you and fun activities for your child. We built this book to be user friendly, so you and your child can fit in some quality time, even as you're juggling all your other parental responsibilities.

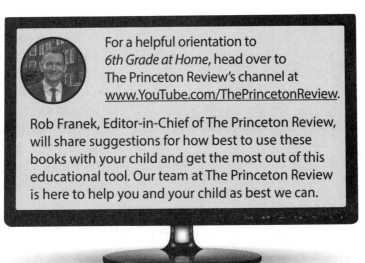

For a helpful orientation to *6th Grade at Home*, head over to The Princeton Review's channel at www.YouTube.com/ThePrincetonReview.

Rob Franek, Editor-in-Chief of The Princeton Review, will share suggestions for how best to use these books with your child and get the most out of this educational tool. Our team at The Princeton Review is here to help you and your child as best we can.

# A Parent's Many Hats

As a parent, we understand you are expected to wear many hats. Check out the following ways you can use *6th Grade at Home* to get more involved in your child's academic life.

**Teacher.** You taught your child how to cross the street and tie his or her shoes. In addition, you may have worked to teach your child academic skills by reviewing the alphabet, helping your child memorize facts, and explaining concepts to your child. By doing so, you are modeling a great learning attitude and great study habits for your child. You are teaching him or her the value of school.

**Nurturer.** As a nurturer, you're always there to support your child through tough times, celebrate your child's successes, and give your child rules and limits. You encourage your child while holding high expectations. All of this can help your child feel safe and supported enough to face challenges and opportunities at school, like new classmates, new teachers, and so on.

**Intermediary.** You're your child's first representative in the world. You're the main go-between and communicator for your child (school-to-home and home-to-school).

**Advocate.** As an advocate, you can do many things: sit on advisory councils at school, assist in the classroom, join the PTA, volunteer in school programs, vote in school board elections, and argue for learning standards and approaches you believe in.

· · · · • • • • • • • • ●

*Sometimes it's hard to know what to do, and it's easy to feel overwhelmed. But remember, it's not all on your shoulders. Research shows that family and close friends all have a huge effect on children's academic success.*

# What's in This Book

## The Skill

Each lesson targets a key sixth-grade skill. You and your child can either work on all the lessons or pick and choose the lessons you want. If time is short, your child can work on an activity without reviewing an entire lesson.

## First Things First

This is the starting point for your child in every lesson.

## Parent's Corner

At the start of each chapter, we address you, the parent, and contextualize the lesson so that you can help your child. We'll share ideas, potential roadblocks, and things to watch out for.

---

### Circles

**C**ircle questions are very common on tests, but luckily they always come down to the same few rules.

Imagine that you are going to make a pizza. You have enough cheese to cover a square 12 inches by 12 inches. However, you want to make a round pizza that is 14 inches wide, plus another 2 inches for the crust. If you don't put cheese on the crust, do you have enough cheese to cover the pizza?

At the end of this lesson, you will be able to:

- identify the radius and diameter of a circle
- find and estimate the circumference of a circle
- find the area of a circle

---

**Parent's Corner**

Can you or your sixth grader draw a perfect circle *free hand*? Challenge each other to draw a circle and then have your student label the radius and diameter. Make sure your sixth grader has memorized the formula for circumference ($C = 2\pi r$ or $\pi d$) and area ($A = \pi r^2$) of a circle, as those formulas are important not only for sixth grade, but well beyond.

---

## Dive Right In!

These are questions or activities for your child to complete independently. Give your child as much time as he or she needs. But if your child takes more than 30 minutes, consider the possibility that they may be having a hard time focusing, be unfamiliar with the skill, or have difficulty with the skill.

---

### Dive Right In!

**Running a Race**

**Directions:** Racing tracks are often curved, but runners need to all run the same distance to the finish line to make the race fair. Study this information, and answer the questions.

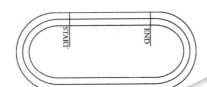

**Explore**
This is where your child can go deeper into the content of the lesson. This section may include explanations, examples, and sample problems. This is what you might call the "meat and potatoes" of the lesson.

# Explore

### The Parts of a Circle

Before we work on circle problems, we're going to need to know the parts of a circle. First off, let's think about what makes a circle special: every single point on a circle is the same distance away from the center of the circle. This distance is called the **radius** of the circle. It is normally represented by an *r*.

**Participate**
Fun, educational activities your child can do with you, family, neighbors, babysitters, and friends at home, in the car, during errands—anywhere.

# Participate

### Activity 1: Adding Punctuation

**Directions:** In 1–3, each sentence is missing one punctuation mark. Rewrite each sentence three times, using a colon the first time, a semicolon the second time, and a period the third time. Then answer questions 4 and 5.

**SENTENCES**

1. Shakespeare is an enigmatic figure no one knows exactly how many plays he wrote.

   a. With a colon:

**Activities**
These may be Hands-On Activities or In-Book Activities. They are an opportunity for your child to try out what he or she has just learned.

### Activity 2: Hands-On

Have your partner/sibling make a list of things he/she will put in a backpack. They don't have to make sense! You could put a walrus in a backpack, right? Write out the list with the correct comma placement!

## One More Thing...

These items are useful tips or facts to keep in mind, or interesting tidbits that are related to the lesson.

Being able to use commas, colons, and semicolons correctly helps you to organize your writing clearly. Without them, your ideas will be jammed together on the page. In particular, knowing how to use colons and semicolons helps you express shades of meaning that you can't express with periods and commas alone.

## In a Nutshell

This is where we review the chapter content. The bullets here will echo the bullets on the front page: this contains the crucial takeaways from this chapter.

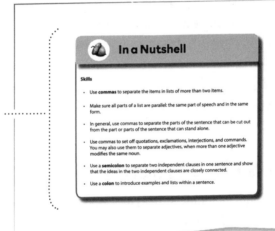

### In a Nutshell

**Skills**

- Use **commas** to separate the items in lists of more than two items.

- Make sure all parts of a list are parallel: the same part of speech and in the same form.

- In general, use commas to separate the parts of the sentence that can be cut out from the part or parts of the sentence that can stand alone.

- Use commas to set off quotations, exclamations, interjections, and commands. You may also use them to separate adjectives, when more than one adjective modifies the same noun.

- Use a **semicolon** to separate two independent clauses in one sentence and show that the ideas in the two independent clauses are closely connected.

- Use a **colon** to introduce examples and lists within a sentence.

## Answers

You and your child can check the answers to the Dive Right In! activities and in-chapter activities. If a question or activity is extremely open-ended, it may not have a specific answer that is "correct." Feel free to discuss the answer with your child and learn how he/she came to that conclusion.

 **Answers for Dive Right In:**

1. The overall topic is therapy dogs.
2. Answers may vary. It takes a special dog to be a therapy dog, and these dogs improve people's lives.
3. Yes.

 **Answers for Participate: Activity 1:**

Student answers may vary.

1. The topic of the first paragraph is a description of therapy dogs.
2. The main idea of the first paragraph is that therapy dogs are dogs that are trained to provide affection and comfort to people in need, such as hospital patients, disaster victims, and retirement home residents.
3. Yes, the other sentences support the topic. Some examples are "Therapy dogs cheer people up by making them laugh, keeping them company, and helping them to relax," and "Just like doctors, nurses, counselors, and rescue workers help people to feel better, so do these exceptional dogs."
4. The topic of the second paragraph is a description of the types of dogs that train as therapy dogs.
5. Many different kinds of dogs are trained to become therapy dogs, but they all have one thing in common: they must have gentle, patient, calm, friendly personalities.

# How Does Your Child Learn Best?

Did you know that your child learns in a lot of different ways? When children learn, they use their minds, their bodies, and their senses—their sense of sight, sound, taste, touch, and smell.

Some children can succeed in any classroom while others need specialized learning support, but all of them have strengths and weaknesses. Your child can learn to rely on his or her strengths and then work on any weaknesses. This book is full of activities that address each of these learning styles.

**Visually—Using Our Sense of Sight**  Your child may learn best by looking at pictures, outlines, maps, and such. Your child may like to draw pictures or take notes.

**Auditory—Using Our Sense of Sound**  Your child may learn best by listening to teachers speak, discussing with friends and classmates, or listening to music while studying. Your child may like to tap a rhythm with his or her pen or pencil while studying.

**Kinesthetic—Using Our Sense of Touch and Movement**  Your child may learn best by moving, taking action, or walking around.

# How to Use Learning Styles

Talk with your child about his or her successes at school, home, or with hobbies. How did your child learn what he or she needed to succeed? Knowing how your child learns best can help you make the most of your child's natural strengths and work on your child's weaknesses.

Once you know how your child likes to learn, you can make sure your child includes those learning methods that work (especially when studying for important tests). You can also support your child as he or she tries out more challenging learning methods. In the long run, this will help your child become a well-rounded learner!

 **The Goal**

You know getting involved with your child's school experiences is the right decision. But here's a reminder of some of the rewards you may reap! Research shows that getting involved in your child's school experiences can result in:

- Increased academic performance

- Better behavior at school

- Increased academic motivation

- Better school attendance

And lest you think your child reaps all the rewards, you might find that helping your child learn gives you:

- More info about your child's school

- A greater sense of your own learning preferences

- More appreciation for all the work you did as a student

- A better relationship with your child's teacher and school staff

# Want to Know More?

Check out these online resources for more reading and math support.

**Math Chimp.** If you want information about more effectively helping your child in mathematics, go to http://www.mathchimp.com.

**Early Math from PBS Parents.** If you want activities to become more engaged in your child's school mathematics program, go to https://www.pbs.org/parents/learn-grow/all-ages/math.

**Parent Resources from Reading Rockets.** If you want to better understand how to enhance parent-teacher conferences and relationships, go to https://www.readingrockets.org.

**Office of Elementary & Secondary Education (OESE).** If you want information about training, advocates, or other educational assistance, go to https://oese.ed.gov.

**Parents for Public Schools.** If you want to find out about chapters of parents working together to advocate for school improvement, go to www.parents4publicschools.org.

**Parent Teacher Association (PTA).** If you want to connect with other parents involved in local schools, go to www.pta.org.

**Parent Training and Information Centers.** If you want to find out about education and services to assist a child with disabilities, go to www.parentcenterhub.org/.

**Reading Is Fundamental.** If you want help with supporting your child's reading and learning, go to www.rif.org.

# English

## Reading

## Writing

## Language

# Finding the Main Idea

**H**ave you ever listened to a friend tell a long story, and found yourself wondering as the friend went on: *What's this story about? What's the point?* Or have you ever *read* a story—or an article or a poem—that made you feel this way? Sometimes what you are reading may seem so confusing that you wish you had the help of a detective like Sherlock Holmes to figure it out! The good news is that you don't need to hire a detective to untangle the message in a story, poem, essay, or article—you just need to know how to find the **main idea**. Then you can do the detective work yourself!

How do you find the main idea? Here is your first clue: in any kind of reading passage, the **main idea** is what the passage is mostly about. It contains the information that an author most wants you to know. Why is this valuable to you as a reader? When you find the main idea, you will find it easier to understand the passage as a whole and you'll better remember the information you read. Finding the main idea will help you in school and on standardized reading tests. It may even help you see the point of your friend's long stories!

At the end of this lesson, you will be able to:

- understand why finding the main idea is important and useful

- develop skills to help you find the main idea

- apply a consistent and step-by-step process to find the main idea

**Parent's Corner**

Sixth graders, when you ask them to tell you the main idea of a newspaper article or book, will often launch into a long-winded summary ("first this happened, then this other thing happened, and then another thing happened...") It can be hard for them to synthesize everything into one clear idea. After you read something with your student, ask them what the three most important details are, and, if possible, have them distill it down to *one* main idea.

# Dive Right In!

## *Marking Up Text*

**Directions:** Read the following passage. Use your pencil to find the main idea and mark it with an "MI." Ask yourself the three questions for finding the main idea and write the answers at the end of the passage.

### Paw Power: Dogs who Bring Smiles and Joy
### Pamela Margid

If you have ever been hurt or sick and had to stay in a hospital, you may have met a very special kind of dog there called a "therapy dog." A therapy dog is a dog that is trained to provide affection and comfort to people who are in hospitals, special needs centers, and retirement homes. They also visit people in disaster areas who have experienced things like floods, hurricanes, or earthquakes. Just like doctors, nurses, counselors, and rescue workers help people to feel better, so do these exceptional dogs. Therapy dogs cheer people up by making them laugh, keeping them company, and helping them to relax. It's hard not to smile when you get a visit from a sweet, furry pup who just wants to be petted, sit with you, and do funny tricks to entertain you.

Many different kinds of dogs work with their human trainers to become therapy dogs. Therapy dogs come in all sizes and breeds, from the tiny Yorkshire Terrier to the great big Golden Retriever. But dogs that are trained to work as therapy dogs have one important thing in common—they all must have the correct personality for the job. To be good therapy dogs, they need to be gentle, patient, confident, and friendly. The dogs must enjoy being around people, being petted, and sitting in people's laps. They need to remain calm in any kind of situation. Before they can visit people and begin their work, therapy dogs must pass behavior tests to make sure they have the right personality for the job. When the dogs in training pass all their tests, they are ready to go to work and make people smile. These days, therapy dogs have become so popular that they even visit schools sometimes, so one day you may meet a therapy dog in your own school—if you haven't already!

## MAIN IDEA QUESTIONS

1. What is the overall topic?

2. What is the most important thing the author says overall about the topic?

3. Do the other sentences support the overall main idea?

*Answers can be found on page 23.*

# Explore

## How to Find the Main Idea in a Paragraph

Let's start by doing some good old-fashioned detective work and taking a look at how to find the main idea in a paragraph. First, you'll need to identify the **topic** of a paragraph.

The topic of a piece of writing tells you what subject an author is writing about. An author separates and begins a new paragraph each time he or she introduces a new topic or idea. This way, each paragraph discusses only one topic or idea at a time. For example, the first paragraph of an essay about President Thomas Jefferson might describe his childhood. *Thomas Jefferson's childhood* would be the topic of that paragraph. Then, the author would start a new paragraph to talk about Jefferson's achievements throughout his life. *Jefferson's achievements* would be the topic of the second paragraph.

Once you identify the topic of a paragraph, you can begin to look for the main idea— the most important point an author wants to tell you about the topic. The author can locate the main idea in different places in a paragraph, but it is almost always found in one sentence within the paragraph. Then, the author uses the rest of the paragraph to discuss the main idea by giving you supporting details.

**Supporting details** are sentences that support the main idea. These sentences contain information in the form of facts, examples, descriptions, or ideas that help explain the main idea. For example, in a paragraph about Thomas Jefferson's achievements, the main idea might be "Jefferson was one of our most talented presidents and he achieved many successes in his lifetime." The supporting details would tell you about some of those achievements—that he was a politician, an architect, an archeologist, an inventor, and the founder of the University of Virginia.

Now that you understand how the topic and supporting details give you important clues about the main idea, let's go find it!

To figure out the main idea, ask yourself these questions as you read:

1.   What is the topic?
2.   What is the most important thing the author says about the topic?
3.   Do the other sentences support that main idea?

When you have found a sentence that answers question 2, you have found the main idea. After finding the sentence that states the main idea, check to see if the details in the other sentences support it. If they do, you can be sure you have found the main idea.

## Use Your Pencil

Your pencil is a useful tool in helping you find the topic, the supporting details, and above all, the main idea, so don't forget to include your pencil in your detective kit! While you are reading, use your pencil to underline the topic and the main idea. When you find the main idea, mark it with an "MI" for main idea. Let's look at an example and try this together.

Read the paragraph below. First, identify the topic. When you've found it, underline it. Then find the main idea. Underline it, too! Mark the main idea with an "MI." Lastly, identify any supporting details. Do the details support the main idea you found?

To double-check your work, ask yourself the three questions for finding the main idea.

⇨        The earth's climate has changed constantly over its 5-billion-year history. In the past, the climate was so warm it caused the oceans to rise and cover much of the earth. At other times, it got so cold that those same oceans froze and covered everything with ice. Both of these changes may seem extreme, but they occurred slowly over many thousands of years. They provide good scientific proof of how the earth has transformed over time.

1.   What is the topic?
2.   What is the most important thing the author says about the topic?
3.   Do the other sentences support that main idea?

In this paragraph:

1. The topic is the earth's climate change. You can tell it is the topic because all the sentences talk about it.
2. The main idea is that the earth's climate has changed constantly in its 5-billion-year history. You can tell that this is the most important thing the author is saying because other sentences describe that idea in detail.
3. The other sentences support the topic because they give you examples of the way the earth's climate has changed over time.

## Finding the Main Idea in a Longer Passage

Now that you are able to detect the main idea in a single paragraph, you can apply what you have learned to find the main idea in a longer reading passage like an article, essay, story, or poem. In a longer reading passage, the main idea is what the *whole* passage is mostly about. It is the *overall* message in an article, essay, story, or poem.

In a longer passage, each paragraph supports the overall main idea. For example, suppose the paragraph that you read earlier about the earth's climate change was part of a longer article called "The Greenhouse Effect." Let's say that the main idea the author wanted to get across was "Due to the greenhouse effect, the earth's climate seems to be heating up much faster in recent years." The main idea in the paragraph you read—that the earth's climate has been changing constantly in its 5-billion-year history—supports the overall main idea of the article that the climate is getting hotter now.

So how do you find the main idea of a longer reading passage? Use the same process you used to find the main idea of a single paragraph. While you read a longer passage, underline the main idea in each paragraph as you find it. Then, when you are finished reading, look at the reading passage as a whole and ask yourself the three questions for finding the main idea:

1. What is the overall topic?
2. What is the most important thing the author says overall about the topic?
3. Do the other sentences support the overall main idea?

When you put all your clues together and ask these three questions, you have all the skills you need to find the main idea in any kind of reading passage!

Let's look at a longer passage from a fictional story and use these three questions to help us find the main idea. Read this passage from *Anne of Green Gables* by L.M. Montgomery. Identify the overall topic of the passage. Then identify the main idea. Using your pencil, underline it and mark it with an "MI." Check to see if other sentences support the main idea that you have identified.

⇨ Matthew feared all females except his sister Marilla and his friend Rachel Lynde. Other than Marilla and Rachel, Matthew found females to be very mysterious creatures. He had an uncomfortable feeling that they secretly laughed at him. Matthew may have been right about that, for he was an odd-looking person! A man of sixty, he had a clumsy figure and long iron-gray hair that touched his stooping shoulders, and a full, soft brown beard that he had worn ever since he was twenty years old. In fact, he had looked clumsy and stooped even at age twenty. The only difference now was that his long hair had turned gray.

When Matthew reached the town of Bright River there was no sign of any train. He thought he must be too early, so he tied his horse in the yard of the small Bright River hotel and went over to the station house. The long platform was almost deserted. The only living creature in sight was a girl who was sitting on a pile of shingles at the far end of the platform. Matthew, barely noting that it WAS a girl, slid past her as quickly as possible without looking at her. If he had looked at her, he would have noticed right away that she was very tense. She was sitting there waiting for something or somebody—and since there was nothing else for her to do there at the station but to sit and wait, she sat and waited with all her might.

Matthew met the stationmaster as he was locking up the ticket office and preparing to go home for supper. Matthew asked him if the five-thirty train would arrive soon.

"The five-thirty train has come and gone a half an hour ago," answered the stationmaster as he hurried to lock up. "But there was a passenger dropped off for you—a little girl. She's sitting out there on the shingles. I asked her to go into the ladies' waiting room, but she told me gravely that she preferred to wait outside. She said it was easier for her to use her imagination and to daydream outdoors rather than here inside the station. She's a strange girl, I must warn you."

"I'm not expecting a girl," said Matthew blankly. "It's a boy I've come for. He should be here. Mrs. Alexander Spencer was supposed to bring him over from Nova Scotia for me."

The stationmaster whistled.

"I guess there's some mistake," he said.

1.  What is the overall topic?

2.  What is the most important thing the author says overall about the topic?

3.  Do the other sentences support the overall main idea?

*Answers can be found on page 23.*

**ONE MORE THING...** If you can quickly find the main idea in any kind of reading selection, reading will become easier and faster. You'll also understand and remember the most important information better. This means that you'll be able to do your reading homework in less time, do a great job with it, and then have time left over! Plus, most reading assignments will ask you questions that require you to identify the main idea. Whether you are taking a reading test in class or you are preparing for a standardized test, your skill in speedily locating the main idea will score you some quick points!

# Participate

## Activity 1: Working Together

**Directions:** With a partner or sibling, use the notes and "MI" markings that you each made for the passage from Dive Right In on pages 10–11 to discuss the following questions. Make sure you both agree on an answer before you write them down.

1.     What is the topic of the first paragraph?

2.     What is the main idea of the first paragraph?

3.     Do other sentences support that main idea?

4.     What is the topic of the second paragraph?

5.     What is the main idea of the second paragraph?

6.     Do other sentences support that main idea?

7. Based on your answers to questions 1 through 6, what is the main idea of the whole passage overall? Does it match what you wrote in question 2 of Activity 1?

8. Does the title of this passage give you any clues about the main idea? Explain your answer.

*Answers can be found on page 23.*

## Activity 2: Hands-On

Think about a movie that you're familiar with and come up with a single main-idea statement about this movie. Then, watch part of the movie and make a list of details in one column that support the main idea. In another column, make a list of details that do *not* support the main idea.

# In a Nutshell

**Skills**

- Identify the topic of a paragraph and that of a longer passage to help you find the main idea in a story, article, essay, or poem.

- Ask yourself, as you look for the main idea: "What is the most important point that the author wants me to understand?"

- Use these questions to help your search for the main idea:

    1.  What is the topic?

    2.  What is the most important thing the author says about the topic?

    3.  Do the other sentences support that main idea?

- Locate the supporting details that agree with the main idea to be sure that you have identified the main idea.

### Answers for Dive Right In:

1. The overall topic is therapy dogs.

2. Answers may vary. It takes a special dog to be a therapy dog, and these dogs improve people's lives.

3. Yes.

### Answers for Explore:

How did you do? Check your answers here.

1. The topic is Matthew's fear of women. You can tell it is the topic because the sentences in the story are about Matthew's fear, especially in the first paragraph where the topic is first introduced.

2. The most important thing that the author wants you to know is that Matthew is uncomfortable around women, and now there's a girl waiting for him at the station instead of the boy he was expecting. You can tell this is the main idea because of the supporting details.

3. The other sentences support the main idea. You can tell they do because they discuss and explain Matthew's fear of women.

### Answers for Participate: Activity 1:

Student answers may vary.

1. The topic of the first paragraph is a description of therapy dogs.

2. The main idea of the first paragraph is that therapy dogs are dogs that are trained to provide affection and comfort to people in need, such as hospital patients, disaster victims, and retirement home residents.

3. Yes, the other sentences support the topic. Some examples are "Therapy dogs cheer people up by making them laugh, keeping them company, and helping them to relax," and "Just like doctors, nurses, counselors, and rescue workers help people to feel better, so do these exceptional dogs."

4. The topic of the second paragraph is a description of the types of dogs that train as therapy dogs.

5. Many different kinds of dogs are trained to become therapy dogs, but they all have one thing in common: they must have gentle, patient, calm, friendly personalities.

6. Yes, the other sentences support the main idea. Some examples are "Therapy dogs come in all sizes and breeds, from the tiny Yorkshire Terrier to the great big Golden Retriever," and "To be good therapy dogs they need to be gentle, patient, confident, and friendly."

7. Therapy dogs are calm, friendly dogs that are specially trained to provide affection, comfort, and entertainment to those in need of cheer, such as people who are ill in the hospital or have been through a disaster. In this sample answer, the main idea is more detailed than that in the previous activity. However, both are valid main ideas. Consider having a discussion about how much detail is appropriate or necessary in a main idea statement.

8. Yes, the title suggests the passage will be about dogs that make people feel better. However, the title does not encompass the whole main idea of the passage.

# Point of View and Author's Purpose

Every time you write something, you have a reason for doing so. You might have to write an essay for a grade, you might write an email to tell your friend what happened over the weekend, or you might just want to express yourself. Professional authors also have a purpose when they write. In this chapter, you will learn to identify what an author's purpose is, and how that purpose affects the writing style.

At the end of this lesson, you will be able to:

- understand the different purposes authors have when they write

- determine an author's purpose

- understand and identify different points of view

- distinguish between an author's purpose, point of view, and tone

**Parent's Corner**

Sixth grade is an important year for students to begin evaluating sources as they dive into doing research for school. Before this year, they might have considered anything written in a book to be "true." Help them to understand how different authors might have a different perspective and how that point of view can drastically affect the quality of the work you're reading. This can also relate to *credibility* in assessing texts. Which resource should we trust more when reading about the surface of the moon: a book published by a NASA astronaut who's spent her whole career researching and observing the moon? or a website published by an anonymous blogger who claims that the moon landing was faked?

# Dive Right In!

## *Just the Facts?*

**Directions:** Three different publications have covered the same topic about exposing children to screen time. Read the articles and determine each author's purpose, point of view, and tone.

**ARTICLE 1.**
**MIT REVIEW, Oct 23, 2019, "Screen Time is good for you—maybe,"**
**Tanya Basu**

In a controversial new study published in the Journal of the American Academy of Child and Adolescent Psychiatry, Andrew Przybylski and colleagues don't just swipe at the predominant thinking that kids should be exposed to as little screen time as possible—they argue that moderate screen time is actually good for kids.

Przybylski, along with his colleagues, found "modest positive relations" when kids used devices and/or watched television for up to two hours a day. Contrary to medical recommendations, the team reported that kids would need to be using screens "for more than five hours a day" before parents would notice any differences.

The study's findings are based on data from more than 35,000 American children and caregivers and reported by the National Survey of Children's Health via the US Census Bureau between June 2016 and February 2017. Przybylski says his analysis suggests that children who are using a digital device—a television, video game console, tablet, laptop, smartphone, or any other gadget with a screen—have better social and emotional skills than kids who don't use this technology.

The research overturns dominant thinking about screen time. Jean Twenge is one of the most prominent critics of letting children have screen time; she argues that technology is making kids less happy. She said in an email she found the study "very strange," particularly because she and her colleagues used the same census data as Przybylski in a paper last year and found the opposite results: heavy screen use led to almost three times the rate of psychosocial issues in kids. Przybylski's interpretation of the same data was that the differences between heavy and light use were small, a discrepancy Twenge said was puzzling.

Nevertheless, Przybylski stands by his findings, calling screen time mandates from health boards "unhelpful, unsupported by evidence, and ... abandoned repeatedly over time."

1.    What is this author's purpose?

2.    What is this author's point of view?

3.    What is the tone of this article?

## ARTICLE 2.
**"Screen Time Recommendations: ECE Experts Shed Light on the Pros and Cons of Screen Time for Kids." Rasmussen College Education Blog, June 3, 2019, Ashley Brooks**

As its name suggests, "screen time" includes everything from video chatting with Grandma to watching cartoons. But not all screen time is equal.

On the one hand, screen time can foster relationships, encourage learning, help develop early literacy skills, and provide early technology savvy: "Phonics plays a huge role in reading, and some kids can struggle with learning the various sounds of the English language. One of the easiest ways for kids to listen to sounds is by watching videos," one expert says. "E-books are also great for children of all ages." In addition, there's no doubt that being technologically capable will remain important in the coming years. Early interaction with screens, especially with the guidance of an adult, can give children a basic understanding of technology that could spark an interest in skills like coding as they grow older.

On the other hand, screen time can cause a lack of social interaction, difficulty paying attention, a delay developmental growth, and even sleep problems. "Babies and toddlers learn through using their five senses. If we think about the senses you use when looking at a screen, you're only accessing your vision and perhaps hearing. You are missing out on the touching, smelling, tasting," a childhood expert says. She recommends balancing screen time with plenty of hands-on activities like playing with blocks, looking at books, pushing a train along tracks, and playing with clay. Furthermore, the National Sleep Foundation reports that "the blue light that's emitted from these screens can delay the release of sleep-inducing melatonin, increase alertness, and reset the body's internal clock to a later schedule." Even high-quality programming or educational apps can disrupt a child's sleep, so experts recommend avoiding all screens in the hours before bedtime.

1. What is this author's purpose?




2. What is this author's point of view?




3. What is the tone of this article?




**ARTICLE 3.**
**"The Harmful Effects of Too Much Screen Time for Kids."**
**verywellfamily.com. Amy Morin, LCSW, September 17, 2020.**

Today's children have grown up with a vast array of electronic devices at their fingertips. They can't imagine a world without smartphones, tablets, and the internet. While digital devices can provide endless hours of entertainment and they can offer educational content, unlimited screen time can be harmful.

Whether you keep the TV on all the time or the whole family sits around staring at their smartphones, too much screen time could be harmful. You may encounter behavior problems, educational problems, obesity, and sleep problems: although many people use TV to wind down before bed, screen time before bed can backfire. The light emitted from screens interferes with the sleep cycle in the brain and can lead to insomnia.

Most of the conversations about the dangers of screen time focus on children. But, it's important to recognize that adults may experience many of the same harmful effects as well, like sleep problems. But even if you aren't experiencing any tangible health problems stemming from your digital device use, there's a good chance your electronics could be harming your relationship with your child.

1.  What is this author's purpose?

2.  What is this author's point of view?

3.  What is the tone of this article?

4.  Do you trust the information in one article more than another?
    Explain your answer.

*Sample answers can be found on page 36.*

# Explore

## Author's Purpose

**Purpose** refers to the reason an author writes a text. Authors write for many different reasons, but these reasons can be placed into three main categories: to inform, to convince, and to entertain. What is the author's purpose in these texts?

1.  Exciting adventures await you in the city that never sleeps! Experience first-rate dining and luxury accommodations as you take in all the breathtaking sights New York has to offer. Lady Liberty is waiting to welcome you. Book your trip now!

    Author's purpose _____

2.  This could happen only to me. If only I hadn't stopped to buy that hot dog! Running to catch the subway, I tripped over my own two feet as I juggled my hot dog, subway map, and cell phone. The hot dog is now in the trash, the map is torn beyond repair, and my cell phone? Well, it made it onto the subway, soaring out of my hands just as the doors were closing. I hope my phone's adventures in New York are better than mine.

    Author's purpose _____

3.  To write the history of Broadway would require a volume, for it would be the history of New York itself. The street was laid out in the days of the Dutch, and began at the Bowling Green. The Dutch called it "Heere Straas," or High Street. The elegant residences between Wall Street and the Bowling Green were once home to a number of famous inhabitants. George Washington himself resided on the west side of Broadway, just below Trinity Church, during a portion of his presidential term.

    Author's purpose _____

Think about other kinds of texts. What's the purpose of a phone book? To inform. What's the purpose of a screenplay? To entertain. Can you brainstorm others?

4.   List at least two examples of writing that are meant to inform the reader.

5.   List at least two examples of writing that are meant to convince the reader.

6.   List at least two examples of writing that are meant to entertain the reader.

*Answers can be found on page 36.*

## Point of View

The author's **point of view** is the way the author chooses to write about the subject. The point of view often includes the author's opinions on the topic. The author's purpose also helps determine the point of view of the passage.

Because authors' points of view will often include their opinions, it is necessary to distinguish between statements of fact and statements of opinion when you read. This is especially important if an author's purpose is to convince the reader.

A fact is a statement that can be proven true. An opinion is a belief that cannot be proven either true or false. Read each of the following statements and decide whether it is a fact or an opinion.

1.   The heart pumps about 1,900 gallons of blood a day.
2.   Artists do not always paint things as they actually appear.
3.   Math is a difficult subject.
4.   There are 60 minutes in an hour.
5.   Dogs are friendlier than cats.
6.   Stories based on real events are more interesting than pure fiction.
7.   Asia is one of the largest continents.
8.   Abraham Lincoln was the greatest American president.
9.   Valentine's Day is in February.
10.   People who steal should go to jail.

In fiction, the point of view describes the type of narrator the author chooses to tell the story. The chart below defines the most common points of view.

| Point of View | Description |
|---|---|
| first person | The narrator is a character who uses "I" or "we." |
| second person | The narrator addresses an audience as "you." |
| third person | The narrator is not a character but describes the actions (and sometimes the thoughts and feelings) of one or more characters using "he" or "she." |

## Tone

Authors carefully choose their words and select specific details to describe a subject. These choices reveal the author's attitude about the subject, the **tone**. To find the tone of a text, examine what words the author uses and ask yourself how the author feels about the subject being described.

Read the following passage from *The Fall of the House of Usher* by Edgar Allan Poe. What tone does Poe use to describe his surroundings and the house? Underline the words that help you determine the tone of the text.

⇨ During a dull, dark, and soundless day in the autumn of the year, when the clouds hung extremely low in the heavens, I had been riding alone on horseback through an especially dreary tract of country. I found myself, as the shades of evening drew on, within view of the melancholy House of Usher. I know not how it was, but with the first glimpse of the building, a sense of unbearable gloom spread through my spirit. I looked upon the scene before me. I looked upon the house and the simple landscape, upon the bleak walls, upon the vacant eye-like windows, and upon a few white trunks of decayed trees. I was filled with an utter depression of soul, which I can compare to no earthly feeling.

**ONE MORE THING...**

Understanding an author's purpose and point of view makes you a more focused reader. For example, if you know the author is trying to convince you of something, you will ask more questions than you might if the text is meant to entertain. Reading with the author's purpose in mind will help you engage with the text so you can respond thoughtfully to test questions or essay assignments.

# Participate

## Activity: Hands-On

Choose three different purposes from the following: to inform, to persuade, to oppose, to defend, to criticize. Make up three different paragraphs and don't change anything, but use a different purpose in each paragraph. Share your writing with a partner or sibling and see if they can guess which purpose you intended!

 **In a Nutshell**

**Skills**

- **Purpose** refers to the reason that author wrote the text. The many reasons authors write fall into three main categories: to inform, to convince, and to entertain.

- The author's **point of view** is how the author addresses the topic. The point of view often includes the author's biases and opinions on the topic.

- **Tone** is the author's attitude toward the subject.

**Answers for Dive Right In:**

Many answers are possible here, but some suggested responses are below:

**Article 1.**

1. The author's purpose is to report the findings of new controversial study that suggests screen time may be healthy for children.

2. The author's point of view is somewhat neutral; the author is giving space to the controversial study, but not necessarily advocating for the study or its detractors.

3. The tone of this article could be described as informative.

**Article 2.**

1. The author's purpose is to give a comprehensive overview about screen time and its effects on children.

2. The author's point of view is balanced quite evenly between the pros and cons of screen time.

3. The tone of this article could be described as informative or neutral.

**Article 3.**

1. The author's purpose is probably to convince the reader that too much screen time is bad.

2. The author's point is view is very much opposed to screen time.

3. The tone of this article could be described as one-sided against screen time.

4. It's up to you which article you trust more! Can you explain, though, why you trust it more than the others?

 **Answers for Explore: Author's Purpose:**

1. Author's purpose: To convince the reader to book a trip to New York.

2. Author's purpose: To entertain the reader with a story about a subway misadventure.

3. Author's purpose: To inform the reader about the history of Broadway.

4, 5, 6. Answers may vary. To Inform: newspaper article, text books. To Convince: advertising, political speeches. To Entertain: novels, screen plays.

 **Answers for Explore: Point of View:**

1. Fact
2. Fact
3. Opinion
4. Fact
5. Opinion
6. Opinion
7. Fact
8. Opinion
9. Fact
10. Opinion

# Literary Elements

**L**iterary elements are used by authors to make their writing more appealing and to give it depth. These devices add layers of meaning to a text the same way an artist adds layers of color to a painting to enhance its beauty.

At the end of this lesson, you will be able to:

- define and understand different literary elements
- recognize literary elements in texts
- identify conflict in literature

**Parent's Corner**

Your sixth grader may not realize it, but she reads and uses literary elements all the time! Try to make this concept more tangible and fun for your student: when you watch a movie together, can you name one or two themes from the story? What about conflict? Challenge your sixth grader, in their own writing, to add more *imagery* to their text; admire how much more interesting a story can be with these literary elements that draw the reader in.

# Dive Right In!

## *Identifying Literary Elements*

**Directions:** Read the following excerpt. Then identify the literary elements in the chart below the poem and answer the questions that follow.

### An Excerpt from "The Raven"
### Edgar Allan Poe

Once upon a midnight dreary, while I pondered, weak and weary,
Over many a quaint and curious volume of forgotten lore[1]—
While I nodded, nearly napping, suddenly there came a tapping,
As of some one gently rapping—rapping at my chamber door.
"'Tis some visitor," I muttered, "tapping at my chamber door—
Only this and nothing more."

Ah, distinctly I remember, it was in the bleak December,
And each separate dying ember brought its ghost upon the floor.
Eagerly I wished the morrow; vainly I had sought to borrow
From my books surcease[2] of sorrow—sorrow for the lost Lenore—
For the rare and radiant maiden whom the angels name Lenore—
Nameless here for evermore.

And the silken sad uncertain rustling of each purple curtain
Thrilled me—filled me with fantastic terrors never felt before;
So that now, to still the beating of my heart, I stood repeating
"'Tis some visitor entreating entrance at my chamber door—

---

[1] Lore means wisdom.

[2] Surcease means ending.

Some late visitor entreating entrance at my chamber door;
This it is and nothing more."

Presently my soul grew stronger; hesitating then no longer,
"Sir," said I, "or Madam, truly your forgiveness I implore;
But the fact is I was napping, and so gently you came rapping,
And so faintly you came tapping—tapping at my chamber door,
That I scarce was sure I heard you"—here I opened wide the door:
Darkness there and nothing more.

Deep into that darkness peering, long I stood there wondering, fearing,
Doubting, dreaming dreams no mortal ever dared to dream before;
But the silence was unbroken, and the darkness gave no token,
And the only word there spoken was the whispered word, "Lenore!"
This I whispered, and an echo murmured back the word, "Lenore!"
Merely this and nothing more.

Back into the chamber turning, all my soul within me burning,
Soon I heard again a tapping, somewhat louder than before,
"Surely," said I, "surely that is something at my window lattice;
Let me see, then, what thereat is, and this mystery explore—
Let my heart be still a moment, and this mystery explore;
'Tis the wind and nothing more."

Open here I flung the shutter, when, with many a flirt and flutter,
In there stepped a stately Raven of the saintly days of yore,
Not the least obeisance[3] made he: not an instant stopped or stayed he;
But, with mien[4] of lord or lady, perched above my chamber door—
Perched upon a bust of Pallas just above my chamber door—
Perched, and sat, and nothing more.

Then this ebony bird beguiling my sad fancy into smiling,
By the grave and stern decorum of the countenance it wore,
"Though thy crest be short and shaven, thou," I said, "are sure no craven,
Ghastly grim and ancient Raven wandering from the Nightly shore—
Tell me what thy lordly name is on the Night's Plutonian shore!"
Quoth the Raven, "Nevermore."

---

[3] Obeisance means a bow or a curtsey.

[4] Mien means appearance.

| Literary Elements | Example from "The Raven" |
|---|---|
| Theme | |
| Setting | |
| Imagery | |
| Plot | |
| Conflict | |

1.    How did you identify the theme?


2.    What category is the main conflict in this poem? What clues in the poem helped you discover it?


*Answers can be found on page 49.*

# Explore

## Types of Literary Elements

Do you have a favorite book? Why do you like it? Is it set in a faraway place? Does it have an interesting main character or villain? Does the story keep you in suspense? The literary elements used in your favorite story are the devices that help to make it more interesting and exciting for you to read.

## Theme

The **theme** of a text is the main idea or message that the author is trying to present. A text can have many different themes. A theme is different from a summary because it shows the greater meaning behind the text instead of reducing it to basic facts. In a story like *Jack and the Beanstalk*, some themes include bravery, deception, and faith in oneself.

## Setting

The **setting** of a text describes where and when the story takes place. Often the setting is used to add to the mood of the story. A scary story would not make the same impression if it took place on a bright and sunny day rather than on a dark and stormy night.

## Imagery

**Imagery** paints a mental picture of something by describing it using the five senses of sight, hearing, taste, smell, and touch. Imagery is a figure of speech. For example, a person in a bad mood can be described as being sour like a lemon. Anyone who has tasted a lemon can imagine the facial expressions of such a grouchy person.

# Plot

The **plot** of a text is the order in which the events of the story unfold. Authors use plot structure to strengthen their stories. Where events are placed within a story can heighten the suspense, create excitement, and provide deeper meaning for the text.

# Conflict

A **conflict** describes the struggle between two different things in a story. Conflicts can usually fit into these five categories:

- person versus self
- person versus person
- person versus society (or community)
- person versus nature
- person versus supernatural (or destiny)

In *Jack and the Beanstalk,* the conflict is person versus person, or specifically, Jack versus the Giant. Jack must defeat the Giant in order to escape and return home.

A story can contain several types of conflict, but there is usually one larger conflict that drives the story. This is called the **main conflict**. The plot of a story grows from the main conflict.

# Literary Elements and Answering Questions

Often during class you won't just be asked to read a passage: you will be asked to write about it or answer questions. Knowing what kinds of literary elements the author has used will help you write about what you've read and answer questions about the text.

Read the fairy tale *Cinderella* below, and then fill in the chart identifying the literary elements within the story. Write in complete sentences.

⇨ There was many years ago, in a faraway kingdom, a gentleman who had a charming lady for his wife. They had one daughter only, who was very dutiful to her parents. But while she was still very young, her mother died, and after a time, the little girl's papa married another lady. Now this lady was proud and stuck-up, and had two daughters as disagreeable as herself, so the poor girl found everything at home changed for the worse. But she bore all of her troubles with patience, not even complaining to her father, and, in spite of her hard toil, she grew more lovely every year.

Now the King's son gave a grand ball, and all persons of quality were invited to it, including Cinderella's stepsisters. Nothing was now talked of but the rich dresses they were to wear.

At last the happy day arrived. The two proud sisters set off in high spirits. Cinderella watched until the coach was out of sight. She then began to cry bitterly. While she was sobbing, her godmother, who was a Fairy, appeared in front of her.

"Cinderella," said the Fairy, "I am your godmother and for the sake of your dear mother I have come to cheer you up, so dry your tears. You shall go to the grand ball tonight, but you must do as I tell you. Go into the garden and bring me a pumpkin." Cinderella brought the finest that was there. Her godmother scooped it out very quickly, and then struck it with her wand, upon which it was changed into a beautiful coach. Afterwards, the old lady peeped into the mouse-trap, where she found six mice. She tapped them lightly with her wand, and each mouse became a fine horse. The rat-trap contained two large rats, which she turned into coachmen. The old lady then told Cinderella to go into the garden and seek half a dozen lizards. These she changed into six footmen, dressed in the finest uniforms.

When all of these things had been done, the kind godmother touched Cinderella with her wand and changed her worn-out clothes into a beautiful ball gown embroidered with pearls and silver. She then gave her a pair of slippers woven of the most delicate spun-glass, fine as the web of a spider.

When Cinderella was dressed, her godmother made her get into the splendid coach, warning her to leave the ball before the clock struck twelve.

On her arrival, her beauty struck everybody with wonder. The gallant Prince gave her a courteous welcome, and led her into the ballroom; and the King and Queen were much enchanted with her. While seated, Cinderella heard the clock strike three-quarters past eleven. She rose to leave, and the Prince asked her to accept an invitation for another ball the next evening.

On reaching home, her godmother praised her for being so punctual, and she agreed to let her go to the next night's ball.

The next evening the two sisters went to the ball again, shortly followed by Cinderella, who was more splendidly dressed than before. Her enjoyment was even greater than at the first ball, and she was so occupied with the Prince's attention that she was not so quick in noticing the passage of time.

To her alarm she heard the clock strike twelve. She fled from the ballroom, but the coach changed again to a pumpkin, the horses to mice, the coachmen to rats, the footman to lizards, and Cinderella's beautiful dress to her old shabby clothes. In her haste she dropped one of her glass slippers and reached home, out of breath, with none of her godmother's fairy gifts except one glass slipper.

When her sisters arrived after the ball, they praised the beauty of the unknown Princess, and told Cinderella about the little glass slipper she had dropped, and how the Prince picked it up. It was evident to all the Court that the Prince was determined to find out the owner of the slipper, and a few days afterwards a royal proclamation was made saying that the King's son would marry the girl whose foot the glass slipper would exactly fit.

This proclamation caused a great sensation. Ladies of all ranks were permitted to make a trial of the slipper, but it was of no use. Cinderella now said, "Let me try—perhaps it may fit me." It slipped on in a moment. Great was the irritation of the two sisters at this; but they were more amazed when Cinderella took the other slipper out of her pocket!

At that moment the godmother appeared, and touched Cinderella's clothes with her wand. Her sisters then saw that she was the beautiful lady they had met at the ball, and, throwing themselves at her feet, begged her forgiveness.

A short time after, Cinderella was married to the Prince, to the intense gratification of the whole Court.

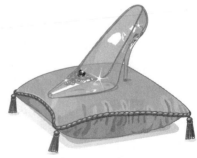

| Literary Elements | Example from "Cinderella" |
|---|---|
| Theme | |
| Setting | |
| Imagery | |
| Plot | |
| Conflict | |

1. What did you find easy about picking out the literary elements in the fairy tale?

2. What did you find difficult? Why?

3. Did recognizing other literary elements help you find the theme of the story? Explain.

*Answers can be found on page 50.*

**ONE MORE THING...** Being able to identify and use different literary elements will help you better understand what you read. It will also help you become a better writer. Writing in a more interesting way will help you write essays, poetry, short stories, and answers to questions on a test. Teachers are more likely to reward students whose writing is strong and exciting.

# Participate

## Activity: Hands-On

Think of an animal you like. With a sibling or friend, write a short story about that animal's life. Try to use as many literary elements as possible; go over the top! Read your stories out loud to your family.

# In a Nutshell

**Skills**

- The **theme** of a story is the main idea or message.

- The **setting** of a story describes where and when the story takes place.

- **Imagery** uses the five senses of sight, hearing, smell, taste, and touch to create a mental picture of a person, place, or object.

- The **plot** of a text is the order in which the events of the story unfold.

- **Conflict** is the struggle between two different elements in a story.

## Answers for Dive Right In:

**Theme:** Sadness can follow you like a ghost. Your mind can play tricks on you when you're scared.

**Setting:** A long time ago, on a dark and spooky night. In a bedroom.

**Imagery:** The tapping, rapping. The darkness. The echoes.

**Plot:** A grieving man hears mysterious noises outside his bedroom late at night. He thinks he may be hearing the ghost of his dead love, Lenore. Instead he finds a raven that speaks to him.

**Conflict:** Person vs. self—the narrator vs. his inner grief and fear

Person vs. supernatural—the narrator vs. the raven/Lenore's ghost

Person vs. nature—the narrator vs. the raven

1. Answers will vary. Be as specific as possible.
2. Main conflict is person vs. self—the narrator vs. his inner grief. The fear he expresses is a major factor in this conflict.

### Answers for Explore:

**Theme:** Good will always win out over bad. Always follow your heart. Remember to be on time.

**Setting:** In a kingdom, far away. Possibly England. A long time ago, during the time of kings and princes.

**Imagery:** The glass slippers were made of spun glass so fine that they were like delicate spider webs.

**Plot:** Cinderella's father remarries a horrible woman after her mother's death. Cinderella wants to go to the ball at the palace. Cinderella's fairy godmother helps her by using magic and transforms her into a noble lady. The Prince falls in love with Cinderella and invites her to another ball. Her fairy godmother transforms her again. Cinderella has such a good time with the Prince that she loses track of time and has to rush out of the palace when the clock strikes twelve. She leaves her glass slipper behind. The Prince finds the slipper and announces he will marry the girl who fits it perfectly. All the women in the kingdom try the slipper. Cinderella asks to try. It fits! She produces the other one. Her stepmother and sisters apologize for being so horrible. She marries the Prince.

**Conflict:** Person vs. person—Cinderella vs. her stepmother

Person vs. supernatural—Cinderella vs. magical spell that ends at midnight

Person vs. society—Cinderella vs. kingdom (She is thought to be too poor to marry the Prince.)

1. Student answers will vary. Possible answers could include plot and setting. Imagery may be more complex and may take students longer to recognize.

2. Student answers will vary. Possible answers may be imagery and conflict. These are more complicated concepts and may take students a few tries to identify them correctly.

3. Student answers will vary, but hopefully students will say yes. Understanding the literary elements in a text helps to reinforce the main idea(s) the author is trying to get across.

# Vocabulary

When you have a good **vocabulary** it means that you know a **plethora** of both commonly used words and less commonly used words. Having a good vocabulary allows you to understand difficult texts and to speak with **aplomb**. In general, having a good vocabulary increases your ability to communicate clearly and efficiently.

At the end of this lesson, you will be able to:

- use strategies that can help you learn vocabulary

- apply vocabulary words in new contexts

- answer questions that use difficult vocabulary

**Parent's Corner**

Vocabulary is a life-long skill that will help your student succeed in school and the workplace. Remember: it's not about impressing other people with fancy words; it's about having access to all sorts of words so you can clearly and effectively express yourself. Having a wider vocabulary can create so many opportunities. Try to use flashcards to quiz your student, and then see if your student can stump *you*! Show them that we are never done learning new things.

# Dive Right In!

## *Vocabulary Expedition*

**Directions:** Read the following passage from Einstein's *Theory of Relativity*. Based only on context clues, write what you think the passage means. Compare what you wrote to what someone else wrote. Answers will vary.

From a systematic theoretical point of view, we may imagine the process of evolution of an empirical science to be a continuous process of induction. Theories are evolved and are expressed in short compass as statements of a large number of individual observations in the form of empirical laws, from which the general laws can be ascertained by comparison. Regarded in this way, the development of a science bears some resemblance to the compilation of a classified catalogue. It is, as it were, a purely empirical enterprise.

But this point of view by no means embraces the whole of the actual process, for it slurs over the important part played by intuition and deductive thought in the development of an exact science. As soon as a science has emerged from its initial stages, theoretical advances are no longer achieved merely by a process of arrangement. Guided by empirical data, the investigator rather develops a system of thought which, in general, is built up logically from a small number of fundamental assumptions, the so-called axioms. We call such a system of thought a theory. The theory finds the justification for its existence in the fact that it correlates a large number of single observations, and it is just here that the "truth" of the theory lies.

# Explore

## The Process of Learning Vocabulary

Why do you need to learn vocabulary? List three reasons.

1.

2.

3.

For this course, every time you come across a mysterious word in any part of a chapter, write that word in your journal. Keep a running list with three columns: Vocabulary Word, Possible Definition, and Dictionary Definition. Based on the context around the word, write down what you think the word means. Next, look up the definition and record a short version of it. Your list should look like this one.

| Vocabulary Word | Possible Definition | Dictionary Definition |
| --- | --- | --- |
| plethora | a lot | a huge amount, a surplus |
| aplomb | knowledge | confidence |
| | | |
| | | |

Unlike some skills, studying vocabulary is an ongoing process. Research has shown that people have to encounter a word five to sixteen times before they really know it.

Here are some ways to study vocabulary. Consider the positives and negatives of each technique. Which ones are most useful for the way you learn? Try each one, and decide which works best for you!

| Ways to Study Vocabulary | Advantages | Disadvantages |
|---|---|---|
| Reviewing with Flash Cards | | |
| Using Mnemonic Devices | | |
| Grouping Words with Similar Meanings | | |
| Learning and Using Roots and Etymologies | | |
| Using Context Clues | | |

# Translating Definitions

Dictionary definitions are only the beginning! Sometimes, dictionary definitions are dry and confusing. Even if you can recite them, you may not actually know what the words mean. Instead of memorizing definitions that mean nothing to you, try this strategy!

First, read the dictionary definition. Then, **translate** the definition into your own words. Your translation should use simple words that are easy for you to understand.

Here's the dictionary definition of a vocab word. Try translating the definition into your own words in the space beaneath it. You may need to look up another word!

un·os·ten·ta·tious adj.: not ostentatious; unpretentious

Now that you've translated the definition into your own words, how are you going to remember it?

**ONE MORE THING...** A good vocabulary is essential to living in society and to communicating effectively. A strong command of the language allows you to do everything from reading a newspaper to completing your taxes. Solid vocabulary allows you to shine in college and job interviews. It gives you more freedom of expression: you can say exactly what you mean by choosing the most precise words.

# Participate

## *Activity 1: Discovering the Meaning*

**Directions:** Go back and reread the previous passage on pages 52–53. Circle all of the words that you don't know. Look up the words, and translate their definitions here. Now that you know the definitions, write what you think the passage means again. Answers will vary.

## *Activity 2: Hands-On*

Read an article in a newspaper and use your pencil to circle all the words you don't know. Look them up and write their definitions on index cards. Ask a parent or friend to quiz you!

# In a Nutshell

**Skills**

- A good vocabulary enables you to understand difficult texts and to communicate clearly and efficiently.

- Record vocabulary words you don't know. Keep a running list with three columns: Vocabulary Word, Possible Definition, and Dictionary Definition.

- Translate dictionary definitions into your own words so that they are easy for you to understand.

# Analyzing a Prompt and Brainstorming

When approaching a writing assignment, the first thing you need to do is analyze the prompt before you begin writing. **Analyzing a prompt** is closely reading the question to determine what sort of response you need to write. A writing prompt may ask you to do a number of things, such as explain a process, tell a story, write a letter, or argue a point.

Once you know what a prompt is asking, you can brainstorm. When you **brainstorm**, write down as many ideas, details, and thoughts that relate to your answer as possible. Imagine a storm going on in your brain with lightning, wind, and rain. A storm isn't organized—it's messy and powerful. When you brainstorm, your goal is simply to write down all the ideas that come to mind. You'll organize them later.

After analyzing a prompt and brainstorming, you'll better understand what the prompt is asking and you'll be better prepared to answer it.

At the end of this lesson, you will be able to:

- determine what a prompt asks and the kind of response it requires
- restate a prompt in answer form
- brainstorm ideas in response to the prompt

---

**Parent's Corner**

When sixth graders receive a writing assignment, they may wish to go with their very first instinct and jump in immediately. It's important to check that your student has considered all possible options in writing topics. Challenge them to brainstorm more and think outside the box! Ask them if their chosen topic has enough examples and supporting evidence to carry the whole essay. In addition, even if they are totally in love with their chosen topic, encourage them to look back and always ask: "does this really respond to the prompt?"

---

# Dive Right In!

## *Analyzing a Prompt*

**Directions:** Read the following prompt. Identify what each sentence in the prompt asks you to do or think about. For each sentence in the prompt, identify what you need to do in order to thoroughly respond. Write this down in your own words in the space following the prompt. Answers will vary.

Think of a piece of art that is important to you. The art could be a painting, a book, a song, or something else. Write an essay that explains why this piece of art is important to you and how it affects you.

# Explore

## Determine What a Prompt Asks

Think about any writing prompts you've read in the past. Most writing prompts are short—they may be a few sentences or a brief paragraph in length. Each sentence in a writing prompt tells you important information about how to best answer the prompt.

When you determine what a prompt asks, read each sentence in the prompt and think about what it is asking you to do. What must you include to completely answer the prompt? Write this down in your own words.

Let's look at an example. Read the following prompt. For every sentence in the prompt, write down, in your own words, what that sentence is asking you to do.

> Imagine that you woke up one day with a special power or skill that you never had before. Write a story about that day. What would that special power or skill be? Would you use that special power or skill and, if so, how?

| Sentences from the Writing Prompt | Analyze Each Sentence |
|---|---|
| Imagine that you woke up one day with a special power or skill that you never had before. | This sentence asks me to . . . |
| Write a story about that day. | This sentence asks me to . . . |

| Sentences from the Writing Prompt | Analyze Each Sentence |
|---|---|
| What would that special power or skill be? | This sentence asks me to . . . |
| Would you use that special power or skill, and, if so, how? | This sentence asks me to . . . |

## Restating the Prompt in Answer Form

Once you have analyzed a prompt, use **key words** from the prompt to prepare to answer it. Key words show the reader of your essay how you are responding and keep you focused on writing a complete answer.

The following examples show how you can use key words from the prompt to start a sentence to put in your essay.

First, underline key words in the two sentences. Then, use the underlined words to write the beginning of your answer.

1.  <u>Imagine</u> that you <u>woke up</u> one day with a <u>special power</u> or <u>skill</u> that you never had before.

    ⇨ If I woke up with a special power one day, I imagine that . . .

2.  Write a <u>story</u> about that <u>day</u>.

    ⇨ Let me tell you about that day . . .

Now, try it on your own:

3. What would that special power or skill be?

   ⇨

4. Would you use that special power or skill, and if so, how?

   ⇨

## Brainstorming

When you brainstorm, you write down *any* thoughts that come to mind in response to a prompt.

Inspire yourself by reading over the prompt and reading what you wrote in your own words when you restated the prompt.

You can also try to answer the following questions: Who? What? Where? When? Why? How? Read the prompt again and write your answers to each question in the spaces provided below.

Who?

What?

Where?

When?

Why?

How?

You can also include details using your sense of taste, touch, smell, sight, and hearing.

Taste

Touch

Smell

Sight

Hearing

Take another look at the prompt. Brainstorm, and write down any other details that come to mind when you consider answering this prompt.

ONE MORE THING... Analyzing a prompt and brainstorming are excellent strategies for answering writing prompts on standardized tests. You can also use these strategies when you are assigned essays in class. Additionally, these skills help you fill out job applications, complete college applications, and answer an interviewer's questions. When you understand a question, you answer more thoughtfully.

Brainstorming is one of those strategies that you can use with everything! What if you don't know what to do for your mom on Mother's Day? You can brainstorm a list of ideas. What if your team doesn't know how to score the winning goal? You and your teammates can brainstorm a list of possible plays to make. You can use brainstorming in countless ways, in all your classes, on tests, at home, at jobs, and with friends.

# Participate

## Activity 1: Restating the Prompt in Answer Form

**Directions:** Now that you have analyzed the prompt on page 62, underline key words in each sentence of the prompt. Then, use these key words to write the beginning of sentences that you can use in your written response. Write the beginning of these sentences in the space below. Answers will vary.

_____

_____

_____

_____

_____

_____

_____

_____

_____

_____

_____

*Answers can be found on page 68.*

## Activity 2: Brainstorming

**Directions:** Now that you have analyzed the prompt, brainstorm ideas to include in your essay. For each question below, write down any ideas, thoughts, memories, details, and information that come to mind. You can use all your senses and answer these questions: Who? What? Where? When? Why? How? Answers will vary.

1.    What is the piece of art?

2.    Describe the piece of art and any memories, ideas, or information you have connected to the piece of art.

3.    Why is the piece of art important to you?

4.    How does the piece of art affect you?

*Answers can be found on page 68.*

## *Activity 3: Hands-On*

Image there is a contest in your town to come up with the best use of a lot that has been sitting empty for years. Do you know of such a place in real life? How could you win this contest? What would be a unique idea for repurposing this space? Collaborate with your sibling or partner to brainstorm some ideas on paper. No idea is too silly! Include any and all ideas. How many ideas can you think of?

# In a Nutshell

**Skills**

- Analyzing a prompt is closely reading a prompt to determine what sort of response you need to write.

- Analyzing a prompt helps you prepare to answer the prompt completely.

- Brainstorm to come up with ideas, thoughts, details, memories, and other information that you can use in your answer. When you brainstorm, you write down anything that comes to mind in response to a prompt.

**Answers for Dive Right In:**

Before you write the essay, analyze the prompt. Make sure to catch that the prompt is not asking you to write about any piece of art, but, rather, a piece of art that is important to *you*.

**Answers for Participate: Activity 1:**

Go back and look at the prompt and underline the most important part. Most likely you underlined the following sentence: "Write an essay that explains why this piece of art is important to you and how it affects you." The word "important to you" should be underlined. Therefore, you shouldn't start your essay by writing "I know about a work of art: a song," because it doesn't address the prompt very well. A better sentence would be something like "A song my mother sings is a piece of art that is important to me." Notice how we're restating parts of the prompt now—success!

**Answers for Participate: Activity 2:**

You may choose to write about any piece of art at all (the *Mona Lisa, A Tree Grows in Brooklyn,* "Uptown Funk" even a public sculpture you admire in your hometown!). Just make sure that *you* connect to the piece of art. You don't want to "fake" it! Choose something you really like talking about; that way, you will sound like an expert in your writing! Above all, make sure your sentences not only describe *what* the piece of art is ("a giant iron sculpture of a polar bear downtown"), but, more importantly, *why* you like the piece of art and *how* it affects you ("the giant polar bear is a comforting object to see downtown, especially when you are having a bad day. I feel like the bear is protecting and smiling at our whole city."). Good luck!

# Developing a Draft

**A** **draft** is an early version of a piece of writing. First, focus on organizing your ideas into paragraphs, and then aim to put your paragraphs in a logical order. This process will help you write your first draft.

At the end of this lesson, you will be able to:

- organize your ideas for an essay

- put your ideas in a logical order

- organize your ideas into paragraphs

**Parent's Corner**

Remind your student that it's always a good idea to have a plan before rushing into any task, especially an essay. Many sixth graders want to start writing immediately, but their writing may stray off-course if they don't have an *outline*. Work with your student to make an outline that will set them up for success!

# Dive Right In!

## *Using a Graphic Organizer to Organize Ideas into Paragraphs*

**Directions:** Read the writing prompt about education below and brainstorm some ideas. Then, work with a partner to organize the ideas into the graphic organizer on the next page. The boxes will guide your paragraph creation. Answers will vary.

⇨ What makes education valuable to you? Do you think students learn more valuable lessons inside the classroom or outside it? Support your answer with examples from your personal experiences.

*Answers can be found on page 82.*

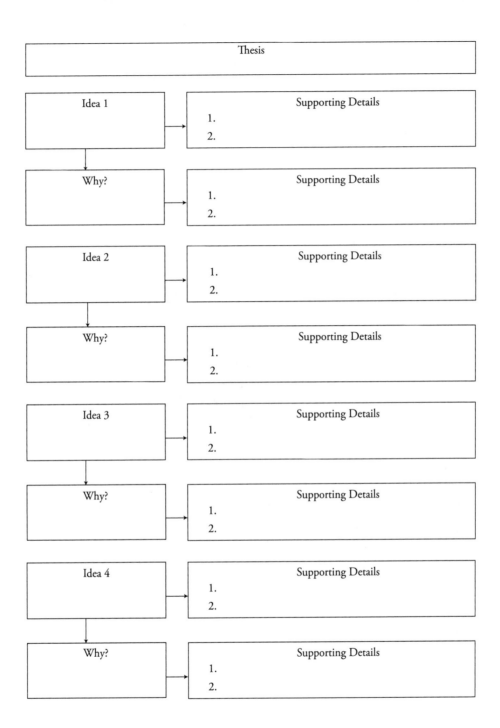

# Explore

## Preparing

**Step 1: Analyze the Prompt.** Closely read the prompt several times. Determine what it is asking you to write.

**Step 2: Restate the Prompt in Answer Form.** Identify key words in the prompt that specify what you should address in your answer. Underline them. Then, use these words to write the beginning of sentences you can use in your essay.

**Step 3: Brainstorm.** Write down as many ideas, details, and thoughts that relate to the prompt as you can. Don't worry about their quality—quantity is more important here! Ask yourself the following questions about the prompt: *Who? What? Where? When? Why? How?* Write down any details gathered from your senses (taste, touch, smell, sight, and hearing).

**Step 4: Write a Thesis Statement.** A **thesis statement** is the point you are arguing in your persuasive essay. It can be debated, but there are facts or experiences supporting it. For example, if you are writing the essay with the purpose of comparing football players to the body, then your thesis might be "The quarterback on a football team is like the brain of the human body." You could support your thesis by describing how both make decisions and direct actions.

# Organizing

Now that you've understood the prompt, written a thesis, and brainstormed a list of supporting details, it's time to organize!

**Step 5: Use a Graphic Organizer.** Organize the ideas in your brainstormed list into a graphic organizer, such as an idea web, a chart, or an outline. Cross out any ideas that are not related to your thesis statement. For each idea, try to come up with a few supporting details. Remember, a detail is a piece of information, a fact, or an experience, so a **supporting detail** gives an example of how or why your idea is true.

**Step 6: Organize Ideas into Paragraphs.** Review the ideas and details in your graphic organizer. If a few ideas or details are related, then you can plan to put them into the same paragraph in your essay. For each paragraph you plan for your essay, identify a **main idea**, or the most important idea you want to express in that paragraph. Make sure that all the ideas and details in that paragraph support that main idea. Each paragraph should have a different main idea.

**Step 7: Organize Your Paragraphs in a Logical Order.** Decide the best order to share your ideas. Then, organize your paragraphs in this order.

There are many ways you can organize your essay. Here are some ways to order your ideas:

- In the order that things happened or should happen
- Identifying all the similarities and then all the differences (or first differences, then similarities)
- Identifying a cause of something, then the effect
- Grouping ideas by category

Check out these examples showing how to order ideas.

| Confusing Paragraph | Ideas about Ordering | Revised Order |
|---|---|---|
| In my favorite dream, I fly a helicopter. I end the day landing on the top of a tall building in the city with crowds clapping. I start out by putting on a helmet. When the sun rises, I zoom over the ocean. | The order of the details doesn't make sense. This paragraph tells a story. So, the paragraph would be clearer if the details were in order from **beginning to end**. | In my favorite dream, I fly a helicopter. I start out by putting on a helmet. When the sun rises, I zoom over the ocean. I end the day landing on the top of a tall building in the city with crowds clapping. |
| **Confusing Paragraph** | **Ideas about Ordering** | **Revised Order** |
| We should have more garbage cans in the park. The park would be a nicer place if there were more flowers. The jungle gym should be fixed. There'd be less garbage on the ground. The park would be a better place for families. | The order of the details doesn't make sense. This paragraph tells causes and effects. So, the paragraph would be clearer if **each cause was paired with its effect**. | We should have more garbage cans in the park. If so, there'd be less garbage on the ground. Also, more flowers would make the park a nicer place. The jungle gym should be fixed. Then, the park would be a better place for families. |

# Putting the Steps Together

Let's follow these seven steps together to write an essay about the following prompt:

⇨  What makes education valuable to you? Do you think students learn more valuable lessons inside the classroom or outside it? Support your answer with examples from your personal experiences.

Now, look at how a student, Tiana, prepared to respond to this prompt by analyzing the prompt and restating each sentence in answer form.

| The Prompt | Step 1: Analyze the Prompt | Step 2: Restate the Prompt in Answer Form |
|---|---|---|
| What makes education valuable to you? | This sentence asks me to define a worthwhile education. | To me, a valuable education is one that... |
| Do you think students learn more valuable lessons inside the classroom or outside it? | This sentence asks me to choose a side about where we learn the most useful stuff. | I think students learn more valuable lessons... |
| Support your answer with examples from your personal experiences. | This sentence asks me to give reasons from my life to argue my answer. | I learned valuable lessons...<br><br>My experience has taught me... |

Now, look at how Tiana prepared to respond to this prompt by brainstorming.

# Tiana's Brainstorm

## What makes an education valuable?

- Gives me tools to have a good career and take care of my family.
- Will bring me success, money, fame, a nice car.

This is Tiana's definition. Yours may be different because you may value different things!

## Lessons from outside the classroom:

- I learn morals and values from my family.
- I learn how to do things I need to do in life (cook, chores, shop).
- Doing chores and getting an allowance teaches me responsibility and the value of money.
- I learn how to interact with friends, family, neighbors, and my community.
- I learn cultural things (language, food, holidays).

Based on Tiana's definition, the lessons she learns outside the classroom are not as valuable to her as an education.

## Lessons from inside the classroom:

- I learn how to succeed in school, which will lead me to college, a good job, money, and the life I want.
- I learn skills like math, reading, and writing. These will be helpful in college and a job.
- I learn how to complete tasks (homework, papers) with a deadline.
- I learn how to take tests (lots of tests in life).
- I learn how to interact with people I normally wouldn't (teachers, different type of students).
- I learn things I wouldn't normally.
- I learn how to do lots of different activities (gym, art, clubs).
- People sometimes challenge the way I think about something, so my mind grows.

Based on Tiana's definition, the lessons she learns inside the classroom are useful and valuable to her as an education. Additionally, she has more examples supporting this argument.

Based on her brainstorm, what do you think her thesis should be? Remember, this is her view, so it may be different from yours!

**ONE MORE THING...**

Planning and organizing your thoughts will help you when you need to respond to a writing prompt. But you can use these skills whenever you want to write clearly and achieve a certain purpose with your writing. Writing a letter to your teacher, writing an email to a company asking for a refund, and writing instructions to a friend to feed your cat are all examples of times when you can use the skills of planning and organizing.

Sometimes you will have a time limit when you write, such as during a standardized test or final exam. You might be worried about using time to plan and organize when you have a time limit. But planning and organizing can actually save you time later—if you already have a plan, then the actual writing will most likely take less time, be more clear, and have fewer errors that you have to fix. So, if you have a time limit, spend a couple of minutes planning and organizing before you begin writing your response.

# Participate

## Activity 1: Organizing Your Paragraphs in a Logical Order

**Directions:** Work with a partner or sibling. Decide the best way to order your ideas from page 72 into a series of paragraphs. Answers will vary.

1.    Discuss different ways to organize the paragraphs with your partner (chronological order, similarities/differences, cause and effect, category or type, etc.). Write your ideas in the chart to the right.

*Answers can be found on page 82.*

| Ways to Order Paragraphs | Pros | Cons |
|---|---|---|
| | | |
| | | |
| | | |
| | | |
| | | |

2. Now, pick one of these ways to organize your paragraphs. Using this order, write your ideas in a new graphic organizer. Be sure to identify the main idea of each paragraph.

| Thesis | |
|---|---|
| **First Paragraph's Main Idea** | |
| Idea 1 | Supporting Details<br>1.<br>2. |
| Idea 2 | Supporting Details<br>1.<br>2. |
| **Second Paragraph's Main Idea** | |
| Idea 1 | Supporting Details<br>1.<br>2. |
| Idea 2 | Supporting Details<br>1.<br>2. |
| **Third Paragraph's Main Idea** | |
| Idea 1 | Supporting Details<br>1.<br>2. |
| Idea 2 | Supporting Details<br>1.<br>2. |

## Activity 2: Hands-On

Imagine you are writing a letter to your local political representative about an issue you care about in your community (a renovated library, repaving streets, a new park in town, etc). Write a first draft of this letter. Remember: your goal is to persuade the representative to see things from your point of view. Don't worry if it's messy—just get something down on the page!

# In a Nutshell

### Skills

- When you organize your ideas, you can use a graphic organizer, such as an outline, idea web, or flow chart.

- Identify related or connected ideas in order to form ideas into paragraphs. After identifying the main idea of a paragraph, you can identify the details that best support that main idea.

- The paragraphs in an essay must follow a logical order.

**Answers for Dive Right In:**

Answers will, of course, vary here. With brainstorming, no idea is too outlandish! Write down whatever comes to your mind. Think about your own life: what has worked best for you in terms of your own education? When do you find that you've really *learned* something? Do you learn best by taking notes and making flashcards? Or do you like to head "into the field" and experience things in nature? Is education useful for learning information, or are there things to be learned, say, in the hallways or cafeteria? The prompt asks for specific examples, so be sure to include a memory from your own education. Was there a time where a group project worked out really well?

*One important tip:* brainstorm any and all ideas, but do not necessarily include every idea in your outline, especially if you cannot think of a specific example. If you have too many brainstorm ideas, narrow it down by choosing only the ideas for which you have several vivid examples!

 **Answers for Activity 1:**

Like with brainstorming, there is no *right* way to order your paragraphs. There are more logical ways, however. You might choose to organize your paragaphs in a chronological order, starting by detailing your kindergarten education and then moving up through the years. If you choose a chronological order, however, make sure you stick with it! Don't jump around from year to year.

You might also choose to organize your paragraphs in a thematic way. Maybe you have three body paragraphs, one about the benefits of in-class education, one about the benefits of group projects, and one about the benefits of outdoor/nature education.

You may also want to include a *counterexample*, an example that goes against your own ideas about education, to create a well-rounded argument. That way, you can give credit to another perspective, but then use your own examples to show why the counterexample is less convincing. In terms of organizing, it's usually customary to start by setting out your own examples and then give a counterexample, rather than opening your essay by giving credit to another perspective.

# Revising, Reorganizing, and Editing

**M**ost writers make mistakes when they write a first draft. When you revise and edit an essay, you review the draft you have written in order to fix any errors and to make improvements.

When revising, look at your essay from a big picture perspective first. Examine the structure of the essay as a whole and then individual paragraphs, sentences, and words. Start by checking the essay as a whole to make sure you completely responded to the writing prompt, followed the five-paragraph format, and are presenting your ideas in the most logical order. After reorganizing, narrow your focus. Check all of your paragraphs to improve transitions, add details, and reorganize ideas. Check all of your sentences to fix any errors in grammar, punctuation, and sentence structure. Finally, check all of your words to make sure they are spelled correctly and capitalized appropriately.

At the end of this lesson, you will be able to:

- understand how to follow a process to revise, reorganize, and edit your essays

- revise and edit drafts of essays

**Parent's Corner**

While it is easy to give into the "one and done" impulse with drafting essays, encourage your sixth graders to spend time with their essay drafts and edit them thoroughly. You will be so thankful you spent the time editing: otherwise you wouldn't have caught that misplaced comma or misspelled word, or, moreover, you wouldn't have seen that the third paragraph fits a lot more naturally as the second paragraph. Don't be afraid to dramatically reorganize your essay: remember that nothing is set in stone; you can always write another draft!

# Dive Right In!

## *Whole Essay*

**Directions:** Read the essay below. Then, answer the Whole Essay questions in the revision chart. Mark the margins for where you will need to revise. Answers will vary.

⇨ The prompt asks me to explain the steps to something i do well and why I'm the best at it. Well, one thing i do is cook macaroni and cheese. No one in my family knows my secret recipe. But if you follow my tips here, you are sure to cook a good-tasting macaroni and cheese.

Use at least three different types of cheeses Many recipes will tell you just to use cheddar cheese. But you'll want to use three or more different types of cheese. I recommend using cheddar along with parmesan, Swiss, and mozzarella. You could also use Monterey jack, Colby, or manchego. The blend of these subtle yet different flavors will really make your macaroni and cheese unique and flavorful.

Also, it's important to get the pasta right. Don't cook the macaroni all the way through or it will be soggy and mushy. Instead, cook it for two minutes less than the time on the package. Be sure to use salted water. I like to add at least two tablespoons of salt into my pasta pot before boiling the water. It doesnt matter whether you use sea salt or iodized salt.

Put the pasta and cheese mixture into small baking dishes meant for individual servings. Some people like to use a big rectangular pan, but I prefer the smaller ones. Then everyone gets enough of the crispy topping. I make my own with breadcrumbs crumbled from old, stale bread. I adds parsley and butter. Then I sprinkel it all generously on top of the baking mixture.

These are just a few of my secret tips. Adding a touch of grated nutmeg makes it smells terific. Topping it off with breadcrumbs gives it a satisfying crunch. Next time you make macaroni and cheese, follow all my tips.

| Questions to Ask Yourself | Answers |
| --- | --- |
| 1. Does the essay answer every part of the prompt completely? | |
| 2. Is the thesis statement clear? | |
| 3. Do the body paragraphs support the thesis statement? | |
| 4. Are the body paragraphs in a logical order? | |
| 5. Does the introduction paragraph present the thesis in an interesting way? Does it prepare you for the ideas and details in the essay? | |

| Questions to Ask Yourself | Answers |
|---|---|
| 6. Does the conclusion paragraph restate the thesis in an interesting way? Does it summarize the most persuasive ideas in the essay? | |
| 7. Does the essay flow smoothly? Are there logical transitions between paragraphs? | |
| 8. Are any ideas in the essay confusing? | |

# **Explore**

## **How to Revise, Reorganize & Edit**

Revising is an essential part of the writing process. When you **revise**, you consider the overall flow and organization of your draft and make changes to improve the writing.

After you have written a draft for a class assignment, put it aside for at least a few hours or a day in order to clear your mind before revising. Of course, this means that you must plan your time well so that you finish the essay well in advance of the due date!

When your mind is clear and you can look at the essay with fresh eyes, you are ready to revise. Pretend you are not the writer of the essay. Instead, imagine you are the person who will eventually read the essay. For example, if the essay is a letter written to the local government, then imagine you are a member of the government.

Start by rereading the writing prompt carefully. Then, follow the steps in this revision chart in order, starting with the big picture and narrowing your scope as you go.

| What to Review: Wide Scope to Narrow Scope | Questions to Ask Yourself |
|---|---|
| **Whole Essay** | 1. Does the essay answer every part of the prompt completely? |
| | 2. Is the thesis statement clear? |
| | 3. Do the body paragraphs support the thesis statement? |
| | 4. Are the body paragraphs in a logical order? |
| | 5. Does the introduction paragraph present the thesis in an interesting way? Does it prepare you for the ideas and details in the essay? |
| | 6. Does the conclusion paragraph restate the thesis in an interesting way? Does it summarize the most persuasive ideas in the essay? |
| | 7. Does the essay flow smoothly? Are there logical transitions between paragraphs? |
| | 8. Are any ideas in the essay confusing? |
| **Paragraphs** | 9. Does each paragraph have a main idea? |
| | 10. Does each main idea have enough details to support it? |
| | 11. Are the sentences in each paragraph in a logical order? |
| | 12. Do the sentences flow well together? Are there clear transitions between them? |
| **Sentences** | 13. Are there errors in grammar? |
| | 14. Are there errors in punctuation? |
| **Words** | 15. Are there spelling errors? |
| | 16. Are there capitalization errors? |

**ONE MORE THING...**

When you revise, you polish your essay into a finished piece. Using the writing process, you take your work from a figment of an idea through various stages to a finessed masterpiece. You can develop confidence in your ability to craft an essay. Once you've finished revising and editing, step back and admire your work! Not only will you be able to appreciate the quality of what you've accomplished, but your readers will also be impressed. Revising and editing can make your ideas brightly shine for any reader to see.

# Participate

## Activity 1: Paragraphs, Sentences, and Words

**Directions:** Reread the essay from page 84. This time, answer the Paragraphs, Sentences, and Words questions in the revision chart. Mark the text for where you will need to revise. Answers will vary.

⇨ The prompt asks me to explain the steps to something i do well and why I'm the best at it. Well, one thing i do is cook macaroni and cheese. No one in my family knows my secret recipe. But if you follow my tips here, you are sure to cook a good-tasting macaroni and cheese.

Use at least three different types of cheeses Many recipes will tell you just to use cheddar cheese. But you'll want to use three or more different types of cheese. I recommend using cheddar along with parmesan, Swiss, and mozzarella. You could also use Monterey jack, Colby, or manchego. The blend of these subtle yet different flavors will really make your macaroni and cheese unique and flavorful.

Also, it's important to get the pasta right. Don't cook the macaroni all the way through or it will be soggy and mushy. Instead, cook it for two minutes less than the time on the package. Be sure to use salted water. I like to add at least two tablespoons of salt into my pasta pot before boiling the water. It doesnt matter whether you use sea salt or iodized salt.

Put the pasta and cheese mixture into small baking dishes meant for individual servings. Some people like to use a big rectangular pan, but I prefer the smaller ones. Then everyone gets enough of the crispy topping. I make my own with breadcrumbs crumbled from old, stale bread. I adds parsley and butter. Then I sprinkel it all generously on top of the baking mixture.

These are just a few of my secret tips. Adding a touch of grated nutmeg makes it smells terific. Topping it off with breadcrumbs gives it a satisfying crunch. Next time you make macaroni and cheese, follow all my tips.

| Area of Focus | Questions to Ask Yourself | | Answers |
|---|---|---|---|
| Paragraphs | 9. | Does each paragraph have a main idea? | |
| | 10. | Does each main idea have enough details to support it? | |
| | 11. | Are the sentences in each paragraph in a logical order? | |
| | 12. | Do the sentences flow well together? Are there clear transitions between them? | |

| Area of Focus | Questions to Ask Yourself | Answers |
|---|---|---|
| Sentences | 13. Are there errors in grammar? | |
| | 14. Are there errors in punctuation? | |
| Words | 15. Are there spelling errors? | |
| | 16. Are there capitalization errors? | |

## Activity 2: Writing the Final Draft

**Directions:** Now that you revised, reorganized, and edited the essay, it's time to write the final draft! Use the next two pages to write the final version. Answers will vary.

_____

_____

_____

_____

_____

_____

_____

## Activity 3: Hands-On

Take out your red pen! In the last chapter you wrote a first draft of a letter to your political representative about an issue you care deeply about. Review your first draft of the letter and give it a thorough edit: check for spelling and grammar, but also for larger structural flaws: maybe an entire paragraph should be moved or deleted altogether. Show off your polished letter to your family or friends!

# In a Nutshell

**Skills**

- To **revise** and **reorganize** a draft of an essay, review your essay looking for ways to improve the flow of ideas, organization, and structure of paragraphs. Make sure that you completely answer the prompt.

- To **edit** a draft of an essay, review your essay looking for mistakes in grammar, punctuation, capitalization, and spelling.

- Work in a logical way, from a wide scope to a narrow scope, by answering the questions in this chapter's revision chart.

# Verbs and Agreement

Every sentence has a **verb**. A verb expresses the action in a sentence. Every verb has a **subject**. The subject tells who or what is doing something; the verb tells what the subject is doing.

For example, in the sentence, "My dog Sam runs after the ball," the verb is *runs*. It expresses the action in the sentence. *Sam* is the subject. It tells who is doing the running.

At the end of this lesson, you will be able to:

- use verbs in the present, past, and future tenses

- make sure a verb agrees with its subject

- identify regular verbs and irregular verbs

**Parent's Corner**

Sixth graders use verbs all day long (to write, to read, to sing, to practice, etc…), but make sure they are always using the correct verb for the *subject*. (e.g. "the dog *barks*," "the dogs *bark*," never "the dog *bark*.") You can help your sixth grader with this lesson by really driving home what a "subject" is. Verify that your student understands the difference between the *topic* (or subject!) of a sentence and the grammatical *subject* (i.e. who or what is doing the action), as students sometimes confuse the two ideas.

# Dive Right In!

## *Verbalize It!*

**Directions:** Think of 10 verbs. For inspiration, a list of verbs follows that you may choose from. Better yet, try to think of you own verbs!

Next, create ten sentences using those verbs. Make sure that some sentences are describing what you did in the past, describing what you are doing now (in the present), describing how you will continue that activity in the future. Challenge yourself by using at least three irregular verbs! Answers will vary.

| | | |
|---|---|---|
| to sing | to dance | to walk |
| to laugh | to talk | to eat |
| to drink | to arrive | to depart |
| to smile | to watch | to think |
| to disagree | | |

**EXAMPLE:** to sing

Yesterday I sang my favorite song at a recital.

**EXAMPLE:** to eat

Every morning I eat two pieces of toast.

**EXAMPLE:** to depart

On Thursday our plane will depart at noon.


Your turn!


1. _____

2. _____

3. _____

4. _____

5. _____

6. _____

7. _____

8. _____

9. _____

10. _____

# Explore

## Verbs for Different Times

In the sentence about Sam the dog, the action takes place right now. But not all actions take place now. Some actions took place in the past, and other actions will not take place until the future. The same verb will take a different form depending on whether the action is taking place now, took place in the past, or will take place in the future. These different forms are called **tenses**.

- Verbs that express action that is taking place now are in the present tense.
- Verbs that express action that took place in the past are in the past tense.
- Verbs that express action that will take place in the future are in the future tense.

Most verbs take a similar form in the past tense. To express the past tense, we add "-ed" or "-d" to the verb (and drop the "s" at the end of the verb, if there is one).

Consider the following sentence, in the present tense:

1.  Jason and Samantha **like** chocolate.

If this event occurred in the past, we add "-d" to the verb:

2.  Jason and Samantha **liked** chocolate.

Now consider this sentence, also in the present tense:

3.  Jason likes chocolate.

If we want to change this sentence to past tense, we drop the "-s" from *likes* and add "-d":

4.  Jason **liked** chocolate.

As you will learn later in this chapter, there are some verbs that take a different form in the past tense, but adding "-ed" or "-d" to a verb is the most common way to express the past tense.

To express the future tense, we don't change the verb. Instead, the word "will" appears before the main verb. As with the past tense, we drop the "-s" at the end of the verb if there is one. So the same two sentences in the future tense look like this:

5. Jason and Samantha **will like** chocolate.
6. Jason **will like** chocolate.

## Verbs Are Agreeable

When a verb has only one subject, we call the subject **singular**. When a verb has two or more subjects, we call the subjects **plural**. Most verbs have different forms for singular and plural subjects. Therefore, a verb must **agree** in number with its subject: a singular verb is used with a singular subject, and a plural verb is used with a plural subject.

The singular form of most present tense verbs has an "s" at the end, while the plural form of these verbs does not have the "-s". This is why Jason and Samantha (plural) *like* chocolate, while Jason alone (singular) *likes* chocolate.

Note that, if the main form of a verb ends in the letter *s* or the letters *ch*, we add "-es" for a singular subject; for example:

7. Jason and Samantha **reach** for the box of chocolates.
8. Jason **reaches** for the box of chocolates.

If the main form of a verb ends in the letter "-y", we replace the "-y" with "-ies" for a singular subject; for example:

9. Jason and Samantha **try** to eat less chocolate.
10. Jason **tries** to eat less chocolate.

Notice that we add an "-s" to make most subjects plural—the exact opposite of what we do for verbs. For example, compare the following sentences:

11. This **cupcake tastes** great!
12. These **two cupcakes taste** great!

Finally, note that because the "-s" drops out in the past and future tenses, agreement generally needs to be considered only for the present tense.

# Not All Verbs Are Regular

The act of changing a verb—for agreement or for tense—is called **conjugation**. Most verbs are conjugated in the same way: we add "-s" or "-es" for singular subjects (or "-ies" to replace the "-y"), we add "-ed" or "-d" for the past tense, and we add "will" for the future tense. Verbs that follow these rules are called **regular verbs**. There are many regular verbs, including the following:

13.    cry, dance, lift, toss, trick

The past tense forms of these verbs are what we expect:

14.    cried, danced, lifted, tossed, tricked

Some verbs, however, do not follow all of these patterns. Verbs that do not follow these patterns are called **irregular verbs**. Most irregular verbs break the general rule for the past tense.

Consider the word *catch*. We do not say that Mohamed "catched" the ball. We say that Mohamed *caught* the ball. Similarly, we do not say that Wanda "speaked" well. We say that Wanda *spoke* well.

Moreover, some irregular verbs don't change form at all in the past tense. We do not say that the Giants *beated* the Jets. We say that the Giants *beat* the Jets. Notice that because the present and past tenses are the same, the sentence is unclear without more information. The sentence "The Giants beat the Jets" could mean that the Giants beat the Jets yesterday, or it could mean that the Giants beat the Jets every time they play.

The following are some irregular verbs:

15.    buy, cast, choose, drink, freeze, cut, quit, spread

The past tense forms of these verbs do not follow the general pattern:

16.    bought, cast, chose, drank, froze, cut, quit, spread

Unfortunately, no single set of rules applies to irregular verbs! You just need to know how a particular irregular verb is conjugated. Luckily, irregular verbs are very common. You may know how to conjugate them already. Do you know the past tense of these common irregular verbs?

Now complete the chart on the next 3 pages to explore past tenses of an assortment of verbs.

| Base Verb | Past Tense | Base Verb | Past Tense |
|---|---|---|---|
| beat | | forget | |
| become | | forgive | |
| begin | | freeze | |
| bend | | get | |
| bet | | give | |
| bite | | go | |
| blow | | grow | |
| break | | hang | |
| bring | | have | |
| build | | hear | |
| burn | | hide | |
| buy | | hold | |
| catch | | keep | |
| choose | | know | |
| come | | lay | |
| cut | | lead | |
| dig | | leave | |
| draw | | lend | |
| dream | | lie | |
| drive | | lose | |
| drink | | make | |
| eat | | mean | |
| fall | | meet | |
| feel | | pay | |
| fight | | put | |
| find | | ride | |
| fly | | ring | |

| Base Verb | Past Tense | Base Verb | Past Tense |
|-----------|-----------|-----------|-----------|
| rise | | stand | |
| run | | swim | |
| say | | take | |
| see | | teach | |
| sell | | tear | |
| send | | tell | |
| show | | think | |
| sing | | throw | |
| sit | | wake | |
| sleep | | wear | |
| speak | | win | |
| spend | | write | |

*Answers can be found on pages 107–108.*

**ONE MORE THING...** When you speak with your friends outside of school, you might not always use perfect grammar, and that's okay. But when you have a job or an interview for a job, it is very important to use formal grammar. Speaking formally will show potential employers you are a professional. Using proper verb forms is one way to show off how well you can speak.

# Participate

## Activity: Hands-On

Verbs are action words. Think of your day today. How many actions did you do when you woke up? Write down all the verbs you can think of that comprise your morning routine.

# In a Nutshell

**Skills**

- A verb expresses the action in a sentence.

- A verb should be in the proper tense: past tense for past actions, present tense for current actions, and future tense for future actions.

- A verb should agree with its subject: a singular verb goes with a singular subject, and a plural verb goes with a plural subject.

- Regular verbs follow the same rules of conjugation. Singular verbs end in "s," "es," or "ies." Plural verbs do not. Past tense verbs end in "ed" or "d." Future tense verbs include the word "will."

- Irregular verbs do not follow the general rules of conjugation, especially to form the past tense.

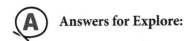 **Answers for Explore:**

| Base Verb | Past Tense | Base Verb | Past Tense |
|-----------|-----------|-----------|-----------|
| beat | beat | forget | forgot |
| become | became | forgive | forgave |
| begin | began | freeze | froze |
| bend | bent | get | got |
| bet | bet | give | gave |
| bite | bit | go | went |
| blow | blew | grow | grew |
| break | broke | hang | hung |
| bring | brought | have | had |
| build | built | hear | heard |
| burn | burned | hide | hid |
| buy | bought | hold | held |
| catch | caught | keep | kept |
| choose | chose | know | knew |
| come | came | lay | laid |
| cut | cut | lead | led |
| dig | dug | leave | left |
| draw | drew | lend | lent |
| dream | dreamt | lie | lay |
| drive | drove | lose | lost |
| drink | drank | make | made |
| eat | ate | mean | meant |
| fall | fell | meet | met |
| feel | felt | pay | paid |
| fight | fought | put | put |
| find | found | ride | rode |
| fly | flew | ring | rang |

| Base Verb | Past Tense | Base Verb | Past Tense |
|-----------|-----------|-----------|-----------|
| rise | rose | stand | stood |
| run | ran | swim | swam |
| say | said | take | took |
| see | saw | teach | taught |
| sell | sold | tear | tore |
| send | sent | tell | told |
| show | showed | think | thought |
| sing | sang | throw | threw |
| sit | sat | wake | woke |
| sleep | slept | wear | wore |
| speak | spoke | win | won |
| spend | spent | write | wrote |

# Pronouns and Agreement

**P**ronouns are words that are used to hold the place of nouns or other pronouns. They're used to make sentences flow more smoothly and more clearly.

It's easy to make mistakes with pronouns because they tend to be small words and are easily overlooked as a result. It's also very common to hear people make mistakes with pronouns while speaking. As a result, there are a number of common mistakes that "sound fine." Because they "sound fine," it's easier to overlook them when writing.

At the end of this lesson, you will be able to:

- identify and edit pronoun agreement errors in sentences

- use subject, object, and possessive pronouns correctly

- use indefinite pronouns correctly

**Parent's Corner**

Pronouns are one of the most misused and misunderstood parts of speech, so if there is one grammar concept to drill with your child, this might be it. Students of all ages use pronouns in their writing and speech, but if you ask your student "what *is* a pronoun?" you may get a variety of responses. Remind your sixth grader of the very simple definition of a pronoun: a word that replaces another word! It's as easy as that.

# Dive Right In!

## *Thank Goodness for Pronouns*

**Directions:** The author of the following paragraph is afraid of pronouns and didn't use any. Please read the paragraph and fill in the correct pronoun wherever appropriate.

### A Really Bad Day

Wes couldn't imagine having a worse day. Wes woke up in Wes's bed early in the morning when Wes's alarm went off. Wes hit the snooze button and rolled over, falling back asleep. An hour later, Wes's mom came running into Wes's bedroom.

"Wes is going to be late for school!" Wes's mom yelled. Wes's mom grabbed Wes's arms and shook Wes awake.

"Oh, no!" Wes said, "Wes just hit Wes's snooze button once! Wes didn't know Wes would sleep so long!"

"Wes had better hurry!" Wes's mom said, as Wes's mom grabbed Wes's clothes out of Wes's drawer. "Shower, then grab some food on the way out."

Wes turned the water on and jumped into the shower.

"Ah!" Wes yelled, "The water is way too cold!"

Wes jumped right out of the shower again. Wes waited until steam started to fill the bathroom, then Wes jumped into the shower again.

"Ah!" Wes yelled, "Now the water is ridiculously hot!"

Wes jumped out of the shower again.

"Forget the shower!" Wes said and put on Wes's clothes. Wes grabbed Wes's books and put them in Wes's backpack. Wes pulled Wes's backpack on, scrambled out the door, and grabbed a piece of fruit from the kitchen.

"Goodbye, Mom," Wes yelled over Wes's shoulder at Wes's mom as Wes went down the street.

*Answers can be found on page 119.*

# Explore

## What is a Pronoun?

A **pronoun** is a word that stands in for a noun. Consider the following sentence:

> **Sanders** is very helpful because **he** always carries the groceries.

**Sanders** is a noun (a person, place, or thing), and **he** is a pronoun that holds the place of Sanders in the second part of the sentence.

Pronouns help you write and speak more concisely. Without a pronoun, the sentence about Sanders would say:

> **Sanders** is very helpful because **Sanders** always carries the groceries.

The second sentence sounds strange, and it's longer.

## Pronoun Agreement: Number

The first rule of pronouns is that they must agree in number with the noun they replace. All nouns are either singular or plural.

The following are singular nouns/pronouns:

1. **Venetia** turned on the hot water. **She** turned on the hot water.
2. **Jose** painted a picture. **He** painted the picture.
3. The **book** fell off the table. **It** fell off the table.

The following are examples of plural nouns/pronouns:

4. The **children** played in the schoolyard. **They** played in the schoolyard.
5. The **birds** sang songs in the trees. **They** sang songs in the trees.
6. I ironed the **shirts**. I ironed **them**.

If the noun is singular, the pronoun must also be singular. If the noun is plural, the pronoun that replaces it must also be plural.

Circle the correct pronoun in the following sentences:

7. Marcus is the best student in the English class. ( He / They ) is the best student.

8. Andrea is the best mathematician I know. ( She / They ) is the best mathematician.

9. Natalia and I are going to the beach. ( She / We ) are going to the beach.

10. Freddie argued for the rule because (we / he ) wants to keep the children safe.

11. Carlos and Rebeka will leave when ( he / they ) get the phone call.

# Pronoun Agreement: Person

It is also important that pronouns agree in *person*. The term *person* in grammar describes who you're talking to or about. *Person* falls into three categories.

When you're talking about yourself, you use the **first person**.

> Example: **I** visited the library today.

When you're talking to someone else, you use the **second person**.

> Example: **You** visited the library today.

When you're talking about someone other than yourself or the person you're talking to, you use the **third person**.

> Example: **He** visited the library today.

Just as nouns and pronouns must agree in number, pronouns must also agree in person.

> Incorrect: When **one** visits the library, **you** should be careful to be quiet.

> Correct: When **you** visit the library, **you** should be careful to be quiet.

> Correct: When **one** visits the library, **one** should be careful to be quiet.

The first example is incorrect because it pairs the third person **one** with the second person **you**. The second and third examples are both correct because the pronouns agree in person.

Please circle the correct pronouns in the sentences below:

1. You shouldn't leave a hot stove unattended when ( one / you ) leave(s) the kitchen.
2. (You / One ) must consider the possibility that your tires need to be replaced.
3. (You / One ) mustn't favor one's friends when making a decision like this.

# Pronoun Agreement: Case

**Case** in grammar describes the function a word plays in a sentence. We are going to consider three kinds of case: subject case, object case, and possessive case.

## Subject Case

Remember that a sentence has to have a minimum of two parts, a **subject** and a **verb**. A **subject** is a **noun** or a **pronoun**, the person, place, or thing that is doing something. A **verb** is an action word, whatever the person, place, or thing is doing. In the following sentences, the *subject* is italicized and the **verb** is bold.

> *I* **go**.
> The *cat* **hunts**.
> *We* **drive**.

## Object Case

The **object** of a verb is also a noun or pronoun. It is the person, place, or thing that the action is being done to. In the following sentences the object is underlined.

> I hit the <u>ball</u>.
> The cat hunts the <u>mouse</u>.
> We drive the <u>car</u>.

Ball, mouse, and car are all examples of **direct objects** because they are all directly affected by the verb. What happens to the ball? I hit the ball.

The other kind of object is the **indirect object**. The indirect object is also a noun or pronoun. It, too, is affected by the verb, but not directly. In the following sentences, the **indirect object** is bold.

> I hit the ball to **Roger**.
> We drive the car to **school**.

Roger is affected by the hitting, but only because the ball is hit *to* him. The school is affected by the driving, but only because we drive the car *to* school.

We use different pronouns for the **subject** and **object**.

> **Roger** hit the ball to **Joel**.
> **He** hit the ball to **him**.

## Possessive Case

We also use a different pronoun to show **possession**. Usually, we add an apostrophe and an "s" to nouns to show possession.

> I hit **Tammy's** ball to Roger.
> We drove **Elise's** car to school.

When we use a pronoun to show possession, however, we don't use apostrophes. Instead, we use **possessive** pronouns.

> I hit **her** ball to Roger.
> We drove **his** car to school.

Here are charts breaking the pronouns down by person and case:

| Singular Pronouns | | | |
|---|---|---|---|
| | **First Person** | **Second Person** | **Third Person** |
| **Subject Case** | I | you | he, she, it |
| **Object Case** | me | you | him, her, it |
| **Possessive Case** | mine | yours | his, hers |

| Plural Pronouns | | | |
|---|---|---|---|
| | **First Person** | **Second Person** | **Third Person** |
| **Subject Case** | we | you | they |
| **Object Case** | us | you | them |
| **Possessive Case** | our, ours | your, yours | their, theirs |

# Possessives

Another type of pronoun is the **possessive pronoun**. The possessive pronoun indicates ownership. They are my, your, his, her, their, and our. For example, in the sentence "Maria twisted her ankle," the word **her** shows that the ankle belongs to Maria. The sentence "Maria twisted my ankle" has another meaning entirely!

Please circle the correct possessive pronoun that could replace the bolded word or words in the sentences below.

Some of these are technically called possessive adjectives, because they DESCRIBE or MODIFY a noun, as opposed to possessive pronouns, which REPLACE or REFER to a noun—but that distinction is not crucial at this moment. As long as you can use these small words properly, the terminology is less important.

1. I borrowed **Tina's** textbook. (**her** / **their**)
2. Jonas bought a copy of **Peter and Mona's** favorite DVD. (**your** / **their**)
3. You shouldn't have taken **the cake that belonged to me**. (**our cake** / **my cake**)

*Answers can be found on page 119.*

**ONE MORE THING...** Pronouns are small words and are easy to overlook. In addition, many people in day-to-day life misuse pronouns, particularly when they're speaking. For this reason, many common mistakes won't sound wrong even though they are, in fact, grammatically incorrect.

For better or worse, people can learn a lot about us by how we speak and how we write. Our writing is clearer when we use pronouns properly. And there are certainly many times when clear, correct writing can help us—on job applications, applications to college, and on tests in school!

# Participate

## Activity: Hands-On

Look around your home and assign pronouns to various things. For instance, your dog Sally is "she," but the waffle maker in the kitchen is "it." How many different pronouns can you come up with?

# In a Nutshell

**Skills**

- **Pronouns** are singular or plural, and must match the nouns or pronouns they replace.

- **Indefinite pronouns** ending in -one, -body, -thing, and -where are singular.

- Some indefinite pronouns can be either singular or plural, depending on context.

- Pronouns have different cases, and must be used accordingly. **Who** is subject case, and **whom** is object case.

- Pronouns can be first, second, or third person voice. They must agree with each other in voice.

**Answers for Dive Right In:**

Wes couldn't imagine having a worse day. He woke up in his bed early in the morning when his alarm went off. He hit snooze and rolled over, falling back asleep. An hour later, his mom came running into his bedroom.

"You're going to be late for school!" she yelled. She grabbed his arms and shook him awake.

"Oh, no!" Wes said, "I just hit my snooze button once! I didn't know I would sleep so long!"

"You'd better hurry!" Wes's mom said, as she grabbed his clothes out of his drawer. "Shower, then grab some food on the way out."

Wes turned the water on and jumped into the shower.

"Ah!" he yelled, "The water is way too cold!"

Wes jumped right out of the shower again. He waited until steam started to fill the bathroom, then he jumped into the shower again.

"Ah!" Wes yelled, "Now the water is too hot!"

He jumped out of the shower again.

"Forget the shower!" Wes said, and put his clothes on. Wes grabbed his books and put them in his backpack. He pulled his backpack on, scrambled out the door, and grabbed a piece of fruit from the kitchen.

"Goodbye, Mom!" Wes yelled over his shoulder at his mom as he went down the street.

 **Answers for Explore:**

**Pronoun Agreement: Number**

7. He
8. She
9. We
10. he
11. they

**Pronoun Agreement: Person**

1. you
2. You
3. One

**Possessive Adjectives**

1. her
2. their
3. my cake

# Adjectives and Adverbs

How do you tell somebody about a person, place, idea, or thing you care about? How do you tell someone exactly what happened at an exciting sports event, as you were walking home after school, or when you saw your friends over the weekend? In all of these cases, you need to find exactly the right words to describe these people, places, things, or events.

Adjectives and adverbs are descriptive words. **Adjectives** modify, or tell more about, nouns and pronouns. **Adverbs** modify verbs, adjectives, and other adverbs.

At the end of this lesson, you will be able to:

- identify adjectives and adverbs

- distinguish adjectives from adverbs

- use adjectives and adverbs correctly

**Parent's Corner**

How can you encourage your student to be more specific in their writing? Adjectives and adverbs can be fun ways to add details and specificity into writing. Sixth grade is an important year to really clarify what adjectives and adverbs are. Ensure that your sixth grader understands the fundamental difference: adjectives modify *nouns*; adverbs modify *verbs*. (Notice that "verb" is in the name "adverb!")

# Dive Right In!

## *Adjective or Adverb?*

**Directions:** Identify whether the following words are adjectives or adverbs. Then write a sentence using each word.

1. good

2. well

3. excellent

4. tasty

5. deeply

6. nice

7. nicely

8. tallest

9. heavily

10. narrow

*Answers can be found on page 128.*

# **Explore**

## Adjectives

Adjectives are words that give more information about nouns and pronouns. In other words, they describe things, people, ideas, and places. The *adjectives* in the sentences below are written in italics.

1. I saw the car.
2. I saw the *red* car.
3. I saw the *black* car.
4. I saw the *fast* car.

The adjectives *red*, *black*, and *fast* describe the car the speaker saw. The word "car" names a thing, so it is a noun and we use adjectives to modify it.

## Adverbs

Adverbs are words that tell more about verbs, adjectives, and other adverbs. Most, though not all, adverbs end in **-ly**. The **adverbs** in the sentences below are written in bold. The first sentence does not contain an adverb.

5. The car drove.
6. The car drove **quickly**.
7. The car drove **slowly**.
8. The car drove **away**.

The adverbs **quickly**, **slowly**, and **away** describe the driving. The word "drove" tells about an action, so it is a verb and we use adverbs to modify it. Notice that although each sentence as a whole tells about the car, the adverbs focus on the action. They tell more about how the car drives.

# Distinguishing Adjectives from Adverbs

Remember that adjectives modify only nouns and pronouns. They describe things, ideas, people, and places. Adverbs modify verbs, adjectives, and other adverbs. Consider the following sentences. The *adjectives* are italicized, and the **adverbs** are in bold.

9.   ADJECTIVE: That is a *slow* car.
10.  ADVERB: That car moves **slowly**.

In the first sentence, *slow* tells us about the car. In the second sentence, **slowly** tells us how it moves. *Slow* tells more about the noun, "car," and **slowly** tells more about the verb, "to move" (or, "moves").

Most of the time, a descriptive word that follows a verb will be an adverb. However, descriptive words that follow verbs that are a form of "to be" (like "is"), or verbs like "to seem," "to look," or "to appear," among others, usually tell about the subject of the verb. The subject of a verb is a noun or pronoun, so the descriptive word is an adjective.

11.  ADJECTIVE: She is *quick*.
12.  ADVERB: She moves **quickly**.

In the first sentence, "is" tells us that *quick*, an adjective, describes the pronoun "she." In contrast, **quickly** is an adverb that tells us how she "moves."

# How's It Going?

To better understand the differences between adjectives and verbs, and to learn to avoid a common mistake, consider the two greetings, "How are you?" and "How's it going?"

When you answer the question, "How are you?" you might say, "I am *good*" or "I am *terrible*." In these cases, you are using an *adjective* to tell how "you" are.

On the other hand, if someone asks, "How's it going?" you might say "It's going **well**" or "It's going **terribly**." In these cases, you are using an **adverb** to tell how it "is going" (a verb).

Many people mix up the adjective *good* with the adverb **well**. They'll incorrectly say, "I'm doing *good*," when they should say, "I'm doing **well**." In this case, the descriptive word tells about the verb, "am doing," so it needs to be an adverb. *Good* is always used as an adjective, so it cannot be used in this case.

However, the word "well" can be used both as an adjective and adverb. So saying, "I'm *well*," isn't necessarily wrong. (Remember, when the verb is a form of "to be," like "am," the descriptive word that follows tells more about the subject of the verb and needs to be an adjective.) However, it is better to say, "I'm *good*" unless you're talking specifically about your health. In other words, saying "I'm *well*" is considered by many people to mean specifically, "I'm healthy."

These mistakes are so common that many people won't notice them. It is best to avoid these mistakes, though, if you're in a conversation with someone whom you'd like to impress.

## More Uses of Adverbs

Most of the adverbs you'll come across will be used to tell about verbs, and so far, all of the adverbs we've looked at have been used to modify verbs. Adverbs can also be used to modify adjectives and other adverbs. Consider the following uses of the adverb **extremely**.

13.    I found Jonas to be **extremely** happy.

Here, **extremely** modifies the adjective *happy*. *Happy* tells us about Jonas, while **extremely** modifies happy, telling us that he's not just kind of happy, he's **extremely** happy. The adverb is modifying the adjective.

14.    The car is moving **extremely** slowly.

Here, **extremely** modifies the adverb **slowly**. **Slowly** tells us how the car is moving, while **extremely** gives us more information about just how slowly the car is moving. In this case, the adverb is modifying another adverb.

 **ONE MORE THING...** Knowing how to use adverbs and adjectives properly helps you to write and speak clearly. Furthermore, knowing the proper use of these words gives you the power to impress people with your knowledge when it comes time to apply for college or for a job.

# Participate

## Activity: Hands-On

Draw a picture based on adjectives you hear from your partner or sibling. For example, the IMPOSING man with the NEON GREEN glasses and SHAGGY, UNKEMPT hair. Then switch partners! Challenge yourself to come up a LOT of adjectives to describe this person.

# In a Nutshell

## Skills

- **Adjectives** modify, or tell more about, nouns and pronouns.

- **Adverbs** modify, or tell more about, verbs, adjectives, and other adverbs.

 **Answers for Dive Right In:**

Students' sentences will vary, but here are some possibilities.

1. adjective; "That is a *good* book."
2. adverb; "You're doing *well.*"
3. adjective; "That is an *excellent* sandwich."
4. adjective; "That sandwich is really *tasty.*" ("Really" is an adverb modifying "tasty.")
5. adverb; "They are *deeply* confused by your question."
6. adjective; "He's a *nice* person."
7. adverb; "He sings very *nicely.*" ("very" is an adverb modifying "nicely.")
8. (superlative) adjective; "She is the *tallest* player on the team."
9. adverb; "She sighed *heavily* when she thought about all her homework."
10. adjective; "The bridge is *narrow.*"

# Commas, Colons, and Semicolons

**C**ommas, **colons**, and **semicolons** are punctuation marks that are used to break sentences up into digestible pieces. Being able to use them correctly will help you to write more clearly.

At the end of this lesson, you will be able to:

- understand and correctly use commas, colons, and semicolons

- identify and correct errors when using commas in a list

- identify and correct run-on sentences and comma splice errors

- identify and correct errors when choosing between semicolons and commas

**Parent's Corner**

There are so many punctuation rules to think about that it can become overwhelming for sixth graders. This is not the time, however, to try to memorize a zillion obscure rules! Reassure your sixth grader that, despite the long list of rules, if you can master just the basics of using these punctuation marks, your writing will be a lot clearer and more effective.

# Dive Right In!

## *Inserting Commas*

**Directions:** Find the list in each of the following sentences. Insert commas where they belong, and make sure the lists are parallel.

1.  I'd like to order a cheese pizza a can of soda and side of garlic knots.

2.  Francine picked up her brother from school made a sandwich and buys a new notebook.

3.  The plan is to find a beautiful park and having a picnic.

4.  He took the set of keys on the table the coat on the hook and the umbrella by the door.

*Answers can be found on page 142.*

# **Explore**

## Commas [,]

The **comma** [,] is used to break a sentence up into manageable pieces. Commas show where to take a breath, or where to pause, in a sentence. Commas are also used in lists and to set apart nonessential parts of sentences.

## Commas in Lists

Commas are used in lists of more than two items. For example:

1.   Correct: Mindy carried her books, lunch, and sweater in her backpack.

This sentence includes a list of three items: *books*, *lunch*, and *sweater*. Notice that a comma goes after each of the first two items in the list. When you write a list of more than two items, include commas after all but the last item in the list. Also remember, commas always go right up against the words that they follow. In other words, don't ever put a space before a comma.

When there are only two items in a list, it is not necessary to use a comma. For example:

2.   Correct: Mary carried her jacket and hat with her to school.

This sentence includes a list of only two items: *jacket* and *hat*. When a list includes only two items, don't separate them with a comma.

# Parallel Lists

Whenever you write a list, all parts of the list must be **parallel**. In other words, each part of the list must be the same part (or parts) of speech and must be written in the same form. Let's look at an example.

3.　Correct: After school, Herman **walks** home, **does** his homework, and **eats** dinner.

This sentence includes a list of three items, each telling something that Herman does after school. The list includes three verbs, all written in the same form: *walk*, *do*, and *eat*. Notice, too, that a comma goes after each of the first two items in the list.

Now let's look at an example of a list with an item that is not parallel.

4.　Incorrect: After school, Herman **walks** home, **does** his homework, and **he will eat** dinner.

This sentence also includes a list of three items, but the last item, *he will eat dinner*, does not look like the others. Whereas the other two verbs, *walks* and *does*, are in the present tense, the last verb is in the future tense. Also, the last item unnecessarily repeats the subject, *he*.

When there are only two items in a list, the items need to be parallel. Consider the following three examples, two of which are correct, and one of which is incorrect:

5.　Correct: My goals are to improve my grades and to become a better writer.
6.　Correct: My goals are improving my grades and becoming a better writer.
7.　Incorrect: My goals are to improve my grades and becoming a better writer.

The first two are correct because items in the list are constructed in the same way. The third example is incorrect because the items are constructed differently.

# Clauses

Because commas are used to break up parts of sentences, let's consider what those parts are.

The main building block of a sentence is a **clause**. A **clause** has a subject and a verb. The following sentence is also a clause:

8.　I came to school this morning.

This sentence is a clause because it includes a subject, *I*, and a verb, *came*. It is considered an **independent clause** because it can stand alone as a complete sentence.

Every sentence must contain an independent clause. An independent clause, though, doesn't have to stand alone. For example:

9.    I came to school this morning after I finished my chores.

In this sentence, *I came to school this morning* is still an independent clause. It can stand alone as complete if you chop off the rest of the sentence.

A **dependent clause**, sometimes called a subordinate clause, is a clause that cannot stand alone. The second part of the sentence above, *after I finished my chores,* is a clause because it includes a subject, *I*, and a verb, *finished*. But it is a dependent clause because it begins with a connecting word, *after*, and cannot stand alone.

Now, consider a part of a sentence that is not a clause.

10.    Coming to school this morning…

This part of a sentence is not a clause because it does not include a subject. It doesn't say who or what is "coming to school."

# Run-On Sentences, Comma Splices, and Semicolons

Two independent clauses stuck together without punctuation form what is known as a run-on sentence. For example:

11.    Incorrect: I go to the library after school it's a good place to do my homework.

This sentence runs two independent clauses, *I go to the library* and *it's a good place to do my homework*, together without anything in between them.

One common but incorrect way to try to fix a run-on sentence is to stick a comma between the two independent clauses.

12.    Incorrect: I go to the library after school, it's a good place to do my homework.

It is incorrect to separate two independent clauses with a comma. This error is called a comma splice.

There are three ways to correct a run-on sentence or comma splice. The first way is to use a period to separate the two independent clauses into two complete sentences.

13.    Correct: I go to the library after school. It's a good place to do my homework.

The second way is to use a **semicolon** [;] to separate the two independent clauses.

14.    Correct: I go to the library after school; it's a good place to do my homework.

A semicolon shows that the ideas in the two independent clauses are closely connected. If you use a semicolon, do not capitalize the beginning of the second independent clause; the two independent clauses are still part of the same sentence. (Notice the semicolon in the preceding sentence!)

The last way to correct a run-on sentence or comma splice is to use a **conjunction** to make one of the clauses a dependent clause. Let's look at an example.

15.    Correct: I go to the library after school because it's a good place to do my homework.

The first part of this sentence, *I go to the library after school*, would still be complete if it stood by itself. The second part of the sentence, *because it's a good place to do my homework*, cannot stand alone. It is a dependent clause. It begins with the **subordinating conjunction** *because*, which tells us that the second part of the sentence is connected to the first.

## Conjunctions and Commas

Conjunctions are words that connect different parts of sentences. Subordinating conjunctions like *because* connect dependent clauses to independent clauses. When a dependent clause follows the independent clause in a sentence, a comma is not needed before the subordinating conjunction. For example:

16.    Correct: I go to the library after school because it's a good place to do my homework.

When a dependent clause comes before the independent clause in a sentence, a comma is needed after the dependent clause. For example:

17.    Correct: Because it's a good place to do my homework, I go to the library after school.

When a dependent clause interrupts an independent clause, commas are also needed before and after the dependent clause. For example:

18.     John's sister, because she's so fast, is an important part of the team.

Coordinating conjunctions can be used to join two independent clauses in one sentence. The coordinating conjunctions are *for, and, nor, but, or, yet,* and *so* (FANBOYS). When a coordinating conjunction is used to join an independent clause to another one, a comma is needed.

19.     Correct: I met your sister yesterday, **and** I found her to be a really funny person.
20.     Correct: She talked to Dan, **but** he didn't have much to say.

Unlike subordinating conjunctions, coordinating conjunctions generally cannot start a sentence.

21.     Incorrect: **And** I found her to be a really funny person, I met your sister yesterday.
22.     Incorrect: **But** he didn't have much to say, she talked to Dan.

## Other Instances in Which to Use a Comma

There are other times when we use commas. For example, we use commas to separate words or phrases that show the order of events when they start a sentence. Consider the following examples:

23.     **First**, pour the pancake mix in the bowl.
24.     **Next**, add water.
25.     **Finally**, stir the mix with a spoon.

Notice that in each case we could cut the time order words and a complete sentence would be left.

We also use commas to separate transitional words from the rest of a sentence, no matter where they appear in the sentence:

26. **Furthermore**, Poe's work created an entirely new genre.
27. Her point, **in addition**, was that these systems must be further explored.
28. No one questioned Rousseau's argument, **in fact**.

Words and phrases like *furthermore*, *in addition*, and *in fact* indicate that the sentence has a relationship with another sentence that came before. Words and phrases like these must be separated from the rest of the sentence with a comma.

We also use commas to separate interjections, exclamations, names of people we're speaking to, and commands from the rest of a sentence. For example:

29. **Wow**, that was probably the best movie I've seen in a long time!
30. That is, **well**, the most beautiful bird in the world.
31. I don't know, **Mr. Agarwal**, if I'm going to be able to repair this vase.
32. **Remember**, you must use commas carefully.
33. You must use commas carefully, **remember**.

Be careful about using interjections and exclamations in your writing. As you can see, they have a more casual tone and are therefore not appropriate for formal writing.

## Commas and Quotation Marks

Another important use of commas is to set off a **quotation**. A quotation tells something that another person said and is surrounded by **quotation marks** [" "].

When using quotation marks, separate the quotation from the part of the sentence that introduces the speaker by using a comma.

34. She said, "I think I'll call Mr. Nguyen after school."
35. "I think I'll call Mr. Nguyen after school," she said.

Notice that the comma that comes before the quotation in the first sentence is outside the quotation mark, with a space separating it from the quotation. The punctuation at the end of a quotation always goes just inside the last quotation mark, with no spaces.

## Separating Adjectives with a Comma

Commas can also be used to separate multiple **adjectives** used with one **noun**. Remember, an adjective is a description word that tells more about a noun, and a noun names a person, place, or thing. The use of a comma in this way is often optional. Consider this example:

36.     The **playful**, **young** monkey climbed the tree.
37.     The **playful young** monkey climbed the tree.

**Playful** and **young** are both adjectives telling more about the noun monkey. With or without the comma, both sentences have the same meaning. Sometimes, however, the use of a comma can clarify meaning. Consider this example:

38.     The **first main** event in the story is the birth of Tina's sister.

This sentence says that the birth of Tina's sister is the first main event, and other main events will follow.

39.     The **first**, **main** event in the story is the birth of Tina's sister.

This sentence tells us that the birth of Tina's sister is the first event in the story. It also tells us that the birth of Tina's sister is the main event in the story.


## The Colon

The primary use of the **colon** [:] is to introduce a list, where the introduction can stand alone as a complete sentence.

40.     Please bring the following items: a toothbrush, soap, and a canteen for water.

It may sound odd, but *Please bring the following items* is, in fact, a technically complete sentence. It doesn't seem to mean much, however, without the list that follows.

Another way to use the colon is when an example follows a complete sentence without a conjunction.

41.     Jessica's friends love to eat pizza: yesterday, they ate two whole pies.

The colon here shows that the clause, "yesterday, they ate two whole pizzas," is an example that demonstrates that Jessica's friends love to eat pizza.

# Participate

## Activity 1: Adding Punctuation

**Directions:** In 1–3, each sentence is missing one punctuation mark. Rewrite each sentence three times, using a colon the first time, a semicolon the second time, and a period the third time. Then answer questions 4 and 5.

### SENTENCES

1.    Shakespeare is an enigmatic figure no one knows exactly how many plays he wrote.

    a.   With a colon:

    b.   With a semicolon:

    c.   With a period:

2.   The presidency is a stressful job the president often sleeps only four hours a night.

   a.   With a colon:

   b.   With a semicolon:

   c.   With a period:

3.   Uta Hagen was an important teacher her classes shaped a generation of actors.

   a.   With a colon:

   b.   With a semicolon:

   c.   With a period:

## QUESTIONS

4.   How does the meaning change as you change the punctuation?

5.   Which style do you prefer for each? Why?

*Answers can be found on page 142.*

## Activity 2: Hands-On

Have your partner or sibling make a list of things they will put in a backpack. They don't have to make sense! You could put a walrus in a backpack, right? Write out the list with the correct comma placement.

## Activity 3: Hands-On

With your partner, alternate one word per person and create a sentence by speaking the words aloud. Try to remember it all and write the sentence down with the correct punctuation. Repeat the game as many times as you'd like!

# In a Nutshell

**Skills**

- Use **commas** to separate the items in lists of more than two items.

- Make sure all parts of a list are parallel: the same part of speech and in the same form.

- In general, use commas to separate the parts of the sentence that can be cut out from the part or parts of the sentence that can stand alone.

- Use commas to set off quotations, exclamations, interjections, and commands. You may also use them to separate adjectives when more than one adjective modifies the same noun.

- Use a **semicolon** to separate two independent clauses in one sentence and show that the ideas in the two independent clauses are closely connected.

- Use a **colon** to introduce examples and lists within a sentence.

**Answers for Dive Right In:**

1. I'd like to order a cheese pizza, a can of soda, and a side of garlic knots.

2. Francine picked up her brother from school, made a sandwich, and **bought** a new notebook. [past tense]

3. The plan is to find a beautiful park and **have** a picnic. [present tense]

4. He took the set of keys on the table, the coat on the hook, and the umbrella by the door.

 **Answers for Participate: Activity 1:**

1. a. Shakespeare is an enigmatic figure: no one knows exactly how many plays he wrote.

   b. Shakespeare is an enigmatic figure; no one knows exactly how many plays he wrote.

   c. Shakespeare is an enigmatic figure. No one knows exactly how many plays he wrote.

2. a. The Presidency is a stressful job: the President often sleeps only four hours a night.

   b. The Presidency is a stressful job; the President often sleeps only four hours a night.

   c. The Presidency is a stressful job. The President often sleeps only four hours a night.

3. a. Uta Hagen was an important teacher: her classes shaped a generation of actors.

   b. Uta Hagen was an important teacher; her classes shaped a generation of actors.

   c. Uta Hagen was an important teacher. Her classes shaped a generation of actors.

4. Responses will vary. Generally, the colon shows that the first part of the sentence is more important, whereas the semicolon and period both make the two clauses seem equally important. The semicolon connects ideas more closely than the period. The colon introduces the supporting information.

5. Responses will vary. Whether or not to use the colon depends on the point you're making. Using a period makes the writing choppier.

# Conjunctions

**C**onjunctions are words that act like directions. Just as you tell a visitor how to go between two different points in your neighborhood, conjunctions tell you how two different parts of a sentence are connected.

At the end of this lesson, you will be able to:

- understand what conjunctions do and where they exist in a sentence

- determine which conjunctions to use in a given sentence

- write and edit sentences using conjunctions correctly

**Parent's Corner**

Conjunctions link words or phrases together. One important topic to review with your sixth grader is how conjunctions work with a complete phrase as opposed to an incomplete phrase. First of all, make sure to review with your student what a *complete phrase* is (a phrase that can stand alone as a sentence; i.e. it has a subject and a verb) and what an *incomplete phrase* is (a phrase that cannot stand alone as a sentence; i.e. it may not have a subject or verb, or it may have a subject and verb but not express a *complete* thought). When your sixth grader reads texts, challenge them to identify which parts of sentences are complete phrases and what parts are incomplete phrases. Additionally, based on that information, can they use conjunctions to link the phrases?

# Dive Right In!

## Creating Sentences

**Directions:** Complete the following sentences. Use a different ending depending on the conjunction.

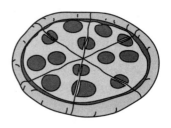

1. Jasper loves to eat pizza, **and**

2. Jasper loves to eat pizza, **but**

3. Jasper loves to eat pizza **because**

4. Jasper loves to eat pizza, **or**

5.　Jasper loves to eat pizza **while**

6.　Jasper loves to eat pizza, **so**

7.　Jasper loves to eat pizza **until**

8.　Jasper loves to eat pizza, **yet**

9.　Jasper loves to eat pizza **unless**

10.　Jasper loves to eat pizza **when**

*Possible answers can be found on page 152.*

# Explore

## Coordinating Conjunctions

**Coordinating conjunctions** are conjunctions that link ideas and words. They tell us about the relationship between two items, and whether those items go in similar or different directions from each other. Consider the following sentences:

1. I ordered a bagel *and* a cup of coffee.
2. I ordered a bagel *but* not a cup of coffee.

*And* tells us that the bagel and the cup of coffee are related and go in the same direction: I ordered both of them. *But* tells us that the two parts of the sentence go in different directions.

The coordinating conjunctions are *for, and, nor, but, or, yet,* and *so* (FANBOYS). Here are some examples of them in action:

3. Jocinda wants to know if she should see the action movie *or* the comedy.
4. Robert would never be late *nor* come to class unprepared.
5. You'll like my friends, *for* they're kind and generous people.
6. The book is interesting *yet* unsatisfying.

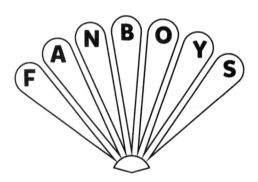

Each of these different coordinating conjunctions tells us about the relationship between two things, and what direction that relationship goes in.

# Subordinating Conjunctions

**Subordinating conjunctions** explain the relationship between ideas in a sentence. They can be used to connect or contrast, or otherwise relate ideas to one another. While coordinating conjunctions can be used to connect words like nouns directly, subordinating conjunctions are used to connect pieces of sentences called **clauses**. Clauses tell us who or what is doing something and what that something is, and they can stand alone as sentences.

Examples of subordinating conjunctions include *because, while, when, if, although, unless,* and *even though,* although there are many more subordinating conjunctions than these. Consider the following two sentences:

> 7. Thomas Edison is recognized as a great inventor. He invented the light bulb and the phonograph, among many other inventions.

As these two sentences are written, they each represent separate ideas. Edison is considered a great inventor, *and* he invented the light bulb and the phonograph, among other things. Written like this, the ideas are equal to each other in importance. By using the word *because,* however, we can create a single sentence and establish a distinct relationship between these two ideas:

> 8. Thomas Edison is recognized as a great inventor *because* he invented the light bulb and the phonograph, among many other inventions.

The word *because* tells us that the second idea is the reason for the first.

A subordinate is someone or something of lower status, less important, or subservient. For example, an employee is subordinate to his or her boss. In this way, the employee is dependent on the boss.

In the same way, the subordinate conjunctions make part of the sentence dependent on the other part. In this case, *because he invented the light bulb and the phonograph, among many other inventions* is now dependent on the rest of the sentence. The first part of the sentence becomes the point, and the second part serves to support the point.

Just as different coordinating conjunctions create different relationships, so too do different subordinating conjunctions:

> 9. Thomas Edison is recognized as a great inventor, *although* his talents as a businessperson are often overlooked.

In the previous example, the word *because* told us that the two ideas went in the same direction. Now, the word *although* tells us that the two ideas go in different directions. Edison's ability as an inventor is recognized; in contrast, his ability as a businessperson is often overlooked.

## Using Conjunctions

Now that you understand what conjunctions are, the key is to make sure you use the right ones. Do you want the ideas to go in the same, or different, directions?

10. *Because* Danielle is an excellent student, Danielle's mom didn't think she needed the extra class.

11. *Although* Danielle is an excellent student, Danielle's mom didn't think she needed the extra class.

Even though these sentences are exactly the same otherwise, their meanings completely change based on which conjunction you use.

**ONE MORE THING...** Conjunctions enable us to write more complicated sentences. In this way we can vary the structure and rhythm of our sentences, and build more complicated relationships between words and ideas. In some cases we wouldn't be able to express our thoughts without conjunctions. However, it's important to use conjunctions correctly so that our ideas are understood!

# Participate

## Activity 1: Choosing Conjunctions

**Directions:** Choose the appropriate conjunctions to form one sentence from each of the following sentence pairs.

1.   Regina is well respected. She is well-liked.

2.   Peter won the science fair. His project was the best one in years.

3.   Natalie's homework paper was thoughtful. It was very hard to read.

4.   Terrence loves to play board games. He didn't want to play games today.

5.   We couldn't sleep last night. Our dog wouldn't stop howling.

6. I met Andrew at the station. His train got in ten minutes ago.

7. Everyone should get a hamster. They make great pets.

8. They eat lots of food. Everyone should get a hamster.

9. Marc and Betty went running. They got tired.

10. You can tell me what you think. I'll keep your thoughts to myself.

*Answers can be found on page 152.*

## Activity 2: Hands-On

Do you have an old essay or writing assignment lying around? Look back through your writing and circle every conjunction you can find. Did you use all those conjunctions correctly? If not, try to rewrite your sentences.

# In a Nutshell

**Terms**

- **Coordinating conjunctions** are used to link words or ideas. They tell us if those ideas or words go in similar or different directions.

- **Subordinating conjunctions** are used to express a relationship between ideas. They explain how those ideas are connected. They connect pieces of sentences called "clauses" that could otherwise stand alone as sentences.

**Skills**

- **Conjunctions** are used to connect words and ideas in your writing. They make your writing more interesting and your sentences more varied. They are particularly valuable when comparing and contrasting things.

**Answers for Dive Right In:**

**There are no wrong answers in this section, really. Below are some possibilities.**

1. Jasper loves to eat pizza, **and** he loves go to the movies.
2. Jasper loves to eat pizza, **but** his mother never lets him.
3. Jasper loves to eat pizza **because** he loves anything with cheese on it.
4. Jasper loves to eat pizza, **or** he wouldn't eat it all the time.
5. Jasper loves to eat pizza **while** taking a bath.
6. Jasper loves to eat pizza, **so** he bought a whole pizza franchise.
7. Jasper loves to eat pizza **until** he gets sick.
8. Jasper loves to eat pizza, **yet** he never actually does.
9. Jasper loves to eat pizza, **unless** it has anchovies on it.
10. Jasper loves to eat pizza **when** it's a full moon.

 **Answers for Participate: Activity 1:**

**Here are some likely responses.**

1. Regina is well respected and well-liked.
2. Peter won the science fair because his project was the best one in years.
3. Natalie's homework paper was thoughtful, although it was very hard to read.
4. Terrence loves to play board games, but he didn't want to play games today.
5. We couldn't sleep last night because our dog wouldn't stop howling.
6. I met Andrew at the station when his train got in ten minutes ago.
7. Everyone should get a hamster because they make great pets.
8. Although they eat lots of food, everyone should get a hamster.
9. Marc and Betty went running until they got tired.
10. You can tell me what you think, and I'll keep your thoughts to myself.

# Math

## The Number System

## Algebra

## Geometry

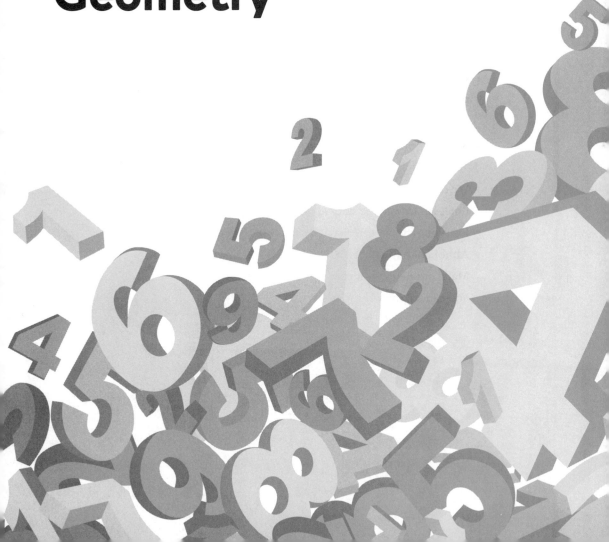

# Working with Fractions

Let's say you order two pizzas but only eat half of one of them. How many pizzas do you have left? You have more than 1 pizza but not quite 2 pizzas. This is where fractions come in. Fractions let us look at numbers that are between the integers. Fractions help you talk about parts of a whole. Another way to write this is $\frac{part}{whole}$.

There are two numbers in each fraction. The top number is the **numerator,** and the bottom number is the **denominator**. That line in the middle means division. A fraction is simply dividing the numerator by the denominator. So if we were to look at the fraction $\frac{6}{3}$, that's the same as $6 \div 3$, which is also equal to the number 2. If we look at the fraction $\frac{1}{2}$, however, $1 \div 2$ doesn't calculate as neatly. Sometimes, like when trying to divide 1 by 2, it's more convenient to leave fractions as fractions. Even in this form, however, fractions are numbers that you can add, subtract, multiply, or divide like any other numbers.

Fractions are simply another way of expressing real numbers. We can also write whole numbers as fractions by dividing by one. For example, 18 in fraction form is $\frac{18}{1}$.

At the end of this lesson, you will be able to:

- reduce fractions
- add, subtract, multiply, and divide fractions
- convert and use mixed numbers

**Parent's Corner**

Adding and subtracting fractions—particularly fractions with different denominators—is one of trickiest math concepts for sixth graders. In later grades, students will have access to a calculator that can solve these questions for them, but it is crucial that they take the time to add and subtract fractions by hand in grade 6.

# Dive Right In!

## *Using Fractions*

**Directions:** With a partner, complete the following exercise. Answers will vary.

First, separately create your own list of six fractions where the numerators and denominators have values between 100 and 200.

1.

2.

3.

4.

5.

6.

Now, trade books. Reduce each of your partner's fractions.

1.

2.

3.

4.

5.

6.

In your partner's book, follow the instructions below, using your reduced values.

7. Add the first two fractions together.

8. Subtract the fourth fraction from the third fraction.

9. Multiply the fifth and sixth fractions together.

10. Finally, trade books again to check your partner's answers.

 # Explore

# Reducing Fractions

If you started with a pizza that has eight slices and four slices are left, what fractional part is left? We can write this in several ways.

4 slices out of 8 or $\dfrac{4}{8}$.

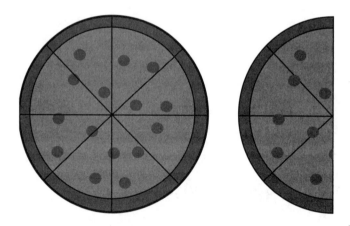

But if you look at the pizza, you realize that half of it is left. So $\dfrac{4}{8}$ must equal $\dfrac{1}{2}$. This is an example of reducing fractions. **Reducing fractions** means getting a fraction into an equivalent form with the smallest possible numerator and denominator. We can do this a little bit at a time or all at once.

As an example, let's look at the fraction $\dfrac{36}{48}$.

First, we need to find a number that divides evenly into both 36 and 48. Because both numbers are even, 2 will work. So we'll divide the top and the bottom by 2.

$$\frac{36 \div 2}{48 \div 2} = \frac{18}{24}$$

As long as we divide both the numerator and the denominator by the same number, we don't change the value of the fraction.

Now we're left with $\frac{18}{24}$. Once again, both the numerator and denominator are even, so we can divide each number by 2.

$$\frac{18 \div 2}{24 \div 2} = \frac{9}{12}$$

Now we've further reduced our fraction.

But looking at $\frac{9}{12}$, we see that only one of those numbers is even, so we can't divide by 2. However, we may still need to simplify further. To find out, we look at other possible common factors.

Let's try 3; 3 divides into both 9 and 12 evenly. So now we divide the numerator and denominator by 3.

$$\frac{9 \div 3}{12 \div 3} = \frac{3}{4}$$

Can we reduce any further? Do 3 and 4 have any common factors (other than 1)? 4 is even, but 3 is not, so we can't divide by 2. 3 is divisible by 3, but 4 is not, so we can't divide by 3. Any number bigger than 3 can't divide 3, so there are no other possible factors. This means that $\frac{3}{4}$ is the most reduced form of $\frac{36}{48}$.

A faster way (although not always the easier way) of reducing fractions is by finding the **greatest common factor** of the numerator and denominator. Let's find all the factors of 36 and 48. To be sure that we find all the factors of a number, we start with the outermost factors and work our way to the middle. The outermost factors of any number are 1 and the number itself. When we come across the same number twice, we've found all the factors.

Let's find the factors of 36.

> Our first pair of factors (the outermost factors) are 1 and 36.
> Is 2 a factor? Yes, because 36 ÷ 2 = 18. So our next pair of factors is 2 and 18.
> Is 3 a factor? Yes, because 36 ÷ 3 = 12. So 3 and 12 is another pair of factors.
> Is 4 a factor? Yes, because 36 ÷ 4 = 9. So 4 and 9 are factors.
> Is 5 a factor? No, so we go to the next number.
> Is 6 a factor? Yes, because 36 ÷ 6 = 6.
> Because we have 6 twice, we know we've found all of the factors of 36.

The complete list of factors for 36 is 1, 2, 3, 4, 6, 9, 12, 18, and 36.

Now let's do the same for 48.

> We begin with 1 and 48.
> We try 48 ÷ 2 = 24 and find that 2 and 24 are factors.
> We try 48 ÷ 3 = 16 and get that 3 and 16 are factors.
> We try 48 ÷ 4 = 12 and get that 4 and 12 are factors.
> We try 5 and find that 5 is not a factor.
> We try 48 ÷ 6 = 8 and find that 6 and 8 are factors.
> We try 7 and find that 7 is not a factor.
> We try 8 and realize that because 8 is already on our list of factors, we have a
> complete list.

The complete list of factors of 48 is 1, 2, 3, 4, 6, 8, 12, 16, 24, and 48.

What's the biggest number on both lists of factors? 12. So 12 is the greatest common factor of 36 and 48. We'll divide the top and bottom by 12. When we do this we get

$$\frac{36 \div 12}{48 \div 12} = \frac{3}{4}$$

Both methods of reducing fractions give us the same answer!

It's up to you which method to use. The one you choose depends on which one looks easier for the fraction in front of you. For the larger numbers, the greatest common factor may be harder to find, so it may be helpful to find smaller factors.

# How to Add and Subtract Fractions

How do we add fractions? If we look at $\frac{1}{2}+\frac{1}{2}$, do we simply add the numerators and denominators to get $\frac{2}{4}$? Well, if we think about it, starting with half of a pizza and adding another half pizza should give us a whole pizza. This method doesn't work because $\frac{2}{4}$ is only half a pizza.

If the denominators are the same, we leave the denominators alone and add the numerators. So $\frac{1}{2}+\frac{1}{2}$ will add up to $\frac{1+1}{2}=\frac{2}{2}$, which equals 1. Similarly, if we wanted to add $\frac{3}{7}+\frac{1}{7}$, we would get $\frac{3+1}{7}=\frac{4}{7}$. The same rule applies to subtraction. If the two numbers we're subtracting have the same denominator, we keep the denominator and subtract the numerators. For example, $\frac{5}{9}-\frac{1}{9}=\frac{5-1}{9}=\frac{4}{9}$.

If the denominators are different, though, we'll have to use a different method.

# Bowtie Method

What happens when we want to add two numbers with different denominators? We'll need to use what's called the **Bowtie Method**. The Bowtie Method allows you to use basic addition and multiplication to add fractions. How would we calculate $\frac{3}{4}+\frac{1}{5}$? Try using the technique you see below.

$$\frac{3}{4} \diagup\!\!\!\!\!\diagdown \frac{1}{5} = -$$

Everywhere you see an arrow, **_multiply_** in the direction of the arrow and write the answer.

First, multiply the denominators. This gives you the new **common denominator**.

$$\frac{3}{4} \diagup\!\!\!\!\!\diagdown \frac{1}{5} = \frac{}{20}$$

Now, multiply diagonally and add the results to find the new numerator.

$$\frac{15 + 4}{\frac{3}{4} \bowtie \frac{1}{5}} = \frac{19}{20}$$

It works every time!

You can use the Bowtie Method on subtraction problems too. The only difference is that you subtract instead of add. Just like any subtraction problem, you simply have to make sure that you keep your numbers in order. Otherwise, you will get the wrong answer.

$$\frac{15 - 4}{\frac{3}{4} \bowtie \frac{1}{5}} = \frac{11}{20}$$

The Bowtie Method can also be used to compare fractions quickly. For example, if we want to know which fraction is bigger, $\frac{3}{5}$ or $\frac{2}{3}$, it's hard to tell by simply looking at them. We'll use the Bowtie Method again, but with one fewer step.

$$\overset{9 \qquad 10}{\frac{3}{5} \bowtie \frac{2}{3}}$$

You don't need to multiply across the bottom when comparing. All you need to do is multiply diagonally. The fraction with the bigger number next to it is the greater one. Because $9 < 10$, $\frac{3}{5} < \frac{2}{3}$.

We can use this method to check that we reduced fractions correctly. For example, we have the fraction $\frac{2}{4}$, and we believe that this reduces to $\frac{1}{2}$. To be sure, we compare the fractions as shown below.

$$\overset{4 \qquad 4}{\frac{1}{2} \bowtie \frac{2}{4}}$$

Because we get a 4 above both fractions, we can confirm that we did, in fact, reduce correctly.

# Multiplying and Dividing Fractions

Not only can you add and subtract fractions, but you can also multiply and divide them. The good news is that multiplying and dividing fractions are actually a little easier than adding or subtracting fractions.

How can we multiply $\frac{2}{5} \times \frac{1}{3}$? All we have to do is multiply the numerator by the numerator and the denominator by the denominator.

$$\frac{2}{5} \times \frac{1}{3} = \frac{2 \times 1}{5 \times 3} = \frac{2}{15}$$

What about division? To divide fractions, we use nearly the same method, but with an extra step. When we divide, we need write the **reciprocal** of the second fraction. The reciprocal is simply the fraction flipped upside down. After we write the reciprocal, we multiply normally. If we wanted to divide the two fractions from the last example, we would calculate in the following way:

$$\frac{2}{5} \div \frac{1}{3} = \frac{2}{5} \times \frac{3}{1} = \frac{2 \times 3}{5 \times 1} = \frac{6}{5}$$

Sometimes when we multiply fractions, we need to reduce. For example, if we were to look at $\frac{20}{6} \times \frac{15}{7}$, we could multiply straight across and get $\frac{300}{42}$. We'd need to reduce this fraction and, as we saw before, it's sometimes difficult to reduce with big numbers. It would be easier to reduce before we multiply, while the numbers are still small. Let's start by reducing $\frac{20}{6}$. Because 20 and 6 are both even, we can divide the top and bottom of our first fraction by 2 and get

$$\frac{10}{3} \times \frac{15}{7}$$

Even though neither $\frac{10}{3}$ nor $\frac{15}{7}$ are in their simplest form, we can still reduce our expression. You don't see how? Well, when we multiply (and only when we multiply), we can reduce not only vertically, but also diagonally. Because 15 and 3 are both divisible by 3, we can reduce even though they're not part of the same fraction. The following equation shows us how this works.

$$\frac{10}{\cancel{3}_1} \times \frac{\cancel{15}^5}{7}$$

This leaves us with $\frac{10}{1} \times \frac{5}{7}$.

Remember, we can only reduce vertically and diagonally. We cannot reduce across. Even though 10 and 5 are both divisible by 5, we can't reduce any further.

Now let's multiply. $\dfrac{10}{1} \times \dfrac{5}{7} = \dfrac{50}{7}$

By using the comparison test below, we can see that our two answers are, in fact, equivalent fractions.

$$\overset{2100}{\underset{42}{\dfrac{300}{}}} \nwarrow \nearrow \overset{2100}{\dfrac{50}{7}}$$

# Mixed Numbers and Improper Fractions

Let's say that you and your friends ordered two pizzas. Each pizza had eight slices, and your friends have eaten three slices total so far. What fractional part of a pizza do you have left?

Well, we started with a total of 16 slices (2 pizzas with 8 slices means $2 \times 8 = 16$ slices). We ate 3 and now have 13 left. Because 13 slices are left and there are 8 slices in one pizza, we have $\dfrac{13}{8}$ of pizza left. A fraction in which the numerator is bigger than the denominator is called an **improper fraction**. All improper fractions have a value that is bigger than 1.

We could also look at this a little differently. We have one whole pizza and 5 slices in a second one. So we could also call this $1\dfrac{5}{8}$. When we write it this way, we call it a **mixed number**.

A mixed number is when a fraction and a whole number are put together. When we write this, $1\dfrac{5}{8} = 1 \times \dfrac{5}{8} = \dfrac{13}{8}$, we'll often need to convert improper fractions to mixed numbers. Here's how we do it.

$$2\dfrac{6}{7} = \dfrac{2 \times 7 + 6}{7} = \dfrac{14 + 6}{7} = \dfrac{20}{7}$$

We always keep the denominator the same. To find the new numerator, we multiply the denominator by the whole number and add it to our original numerator. In the above example, we calculated that $2\dfrac{6}{7}$ is the same as $\dfrac{20}{7}$.

We'll also need to convert improper fractions into mixed numbers. To do this, we need to remember that the fraction bar means division.

In order to convert the improper fraction $\dfrac{63}{5}$ into a mixed number, we must first calculate $63 \div 5$ using long division to find the remainder.

$$
\begin{array}{r}
12\text{r}3 \\
5\overline{)\ 63} \\
5 \\
\hline
13 \\
10 \\
\hline
3
\end{array}
$$

We keep the same denominator from our original fraction. We move our answer, 12, to the whole number place. Finally, we make the remainder our numerator and find that $\dfrac{63}{5} = 12\dfrac{3}{5}$.

## Working with Negative Fractions

We've been looking at fraction problems in which all the fractions were positive. What would we do if we came across a question like this?

$$-\frac{2}{5} + \frac{3}{8}$$

This looks a lot harder than it actually is. If you're comfortable doing math with negative integers, you'll be able to handle negative fractions. All you need to do is move the negative sign to the numerator.

$$\frac{-2}{5} + \frac{3}{8}$$

Then use the Bowtie Method the same way we would for any question.

$$
\overset{-16\ +\ 15}{\frac{-2}{5} \times \frac{3}{8}} = \frac{-1}{40} = -\frac{1}{40}
$$

Use the same trick for multiplication.

$$-\frac{2}{5} \times \frac{3}{8} = \frac{-2}{5} \times \frac{3}{8} =$$

Before we go any further, remember to reduce. In this example, we can only reduce diagonally. Because 8 and –2 are both divisible by 2, we can reduce them and then multiply.

$$\frac{-1}{5}\times\frac{3}{4}=\frac{-3}{20}=-\frac{3}{20}$$

So again, with negative fractions, move the negative sign to the numerator, and calculate the equation as you would a regular fraction.

When we're working with negative mixed numbers and improper fractions, we work as if we there isn't a negative sign and reapply the negative sign at the end.

Let's turn $-3\frac{4}{5}$ into an improper fraction.

$$3\frac{4}{5}=\frac{3\times5+4}{5}=\frac{19}{5}$$

$$-3\frac{4}{5}=-\frac{19}{5}$$

We do the same thing in order to convert improper fractions into mixed numbers. We saw in our example from the last section that $\frac{63}{5}=12\frac{3}{5}$. This means that $-\frac{63}{5}=-12\frac{3}{5}$.

That's all there is to it.

**ONE MORE THING...** Knowing how to work with fractions will help you to solve many problems, from converting recipes to understanding store discounts. For example, if you had a quarter-cup measuring spoon and your recipe called for one cup of sugar, you would know that you need to use your measuring spoon four times. If you went into a store advertising a half-off sale, you would know that the $50 shirt you like is now $25. Fractions are among the most useful math skills you will ever learn!

# Participate

## Activity: Hands-On

Work with a parent or other adult to use this recipe to make cereal bars. Measure the following in $\frac{1}{4}$-cup measuring cups: $\frac{1}{2}$ cup sugar, $\frac{4}{4}$ cup brown sugar, $1\frac{1}{4}$ cups corn syrup, $1\frac{1}{2}$ cups peanut butter, and 6 cups cereal. First, figure out how many $\frac{1}{4}$ cups go into each measurement, and then have your parent or an adult microwave the sugar and corn syrup. Mix in the peanut butter and stir until it's smooth. Lastly, mix in the cereal. You'll need to pour this mixture into a baking dish and even it out. Then, cut into equal bars and refrigerate. Serve when solid.

# In a Nutshell

**Skills**

- Use the **Bowtie Method** to add or subtract fractions.

$$\frac{3}{4} \diagdown\!\!\!\!\!\times\!\!\!\!\!\diagup \frac{1}{5} =$$

- When you multiply fractions, you multiply straight across the numerator and denominator. To divide, you write the reciprocal of the second fraction and then multiply normally.

# Percents, Ratios, and Proportions

**P**ercents, ratios, and proportions are everywhere. We see percents when we buy items on sale such as a shirt that is 25% off. We use ratios when we bake—the amounts listed in a recipe tell us how much of each ingredient we have to use. And we use proportions to figure out how much of something we need based on its relationship to something else. All of these ideas have one thing in common: they all deal to some degree with parts.

At the end of this lesson, you will be able to:

- find percents of a number

- create ratios to describe relationships

- use proportions to work percents and ratios

---

**Parent's Corner**

Help your students understand the important difference between fractions and ratios. While fractions represent a part out of the whole, ratios represent a part in relation to another *part*. A fraction of $\frac{4}{5}$ implies that the whole is five parts, and we've taken up four of those parts. A 4:5 ratio implies that the whole is nine parts ( 4+ 5) and that there are four parts for every five parts. Keep drilling this distinction with your student!

---

# Dive Right In!

## *Survey Your Family*

**Directions:** Select your favorite color out of the choices below, and share your answers. Record everyone's answers in the chart below, and then answer the questions. Answers will vary.

| Favorite Color | Red | Orange | Yellow | Green | Blue | Purple |
|---|---|---|---|---|---|---|
| Number of People in your Home Who Picked It | | | | | | |

1.  How many total people are in your family?


2.  What percent of people chose blue?


3.  What percent of people chose either red or orange?

4.   What is the ratio of the number of people who chose purple to the number of people who chose green?




5.   What is the ratio of the number of people who chose the most popular color to the number of people who chose the least popular color?




6.   If there were three times as many people in your family, but the ratio of yellow to blue stayed the same, how many people would choose yellow? Blue?




7.   If there were twice as many people in your family, but the ratio of red to green to purple stayed the same, how many people would choose each color?

# **Explore**

## **Percents**

Percent means "divided by 100." A **percent** tells you how much you have of something, so it expresses the same relationship as a fraction, which is $\frac{part}{whole}$. The difference is that a percent always has 100 in the denominator. Here are two examples:

$$50\% = \frac{50}{100}$$

$$75\% = \frac{75}{100}$$

## **Percents as Decimals**

You can also write percents as decimals. To convert a percent to a decimal, take away the percent sign, and move the decimal two places to the left.

$$25\% = .25$$

To convert a decimal to a percent, move the decimal two places to the right, and add the percent sign.

$$.45 = 45\%$$

# Percents as Fractions

The difference between fractions and percents is that a percent always has 100 in the denominator. But when a percent has a decimal, we need to add extra zeros to the denominator to make sure that we are representing the correct place value in the fraction.

When we want to write 13.4% as a fraction, we are first going to move the decimal to the right of the number. In 13.4% we can only move the decimal one place to the right to get 134. 134 will be our numerator. To write the denominator, we will add one more zero to 100, because we moved the decimal one place. The denominator will go from 100 to 1,000.

$$13.4\% = \frac{134}{1000}$$

# Finding the Percent of Numbers

Finding the percent of a number means that you're finding some part of a whole.

Let's say you've baked cupcakes for a bake sale and now you're ready to frost them. You can use either vanilla or strawberry frosting. If you baked 30 cupcakes and want 40% of them to have strawberry frosting, how many cupcakes will you need to frost with strawberry frosting?

We'll use the fractional version of the percent to set up this problem. You have 30 cupcakes, which means you need 40% of 30 to be frosted with strawberry.

When you translate words into math, the word *of* means multiply. So here's what you have:

$$\frac{40}{100} \times 30 = 12$$

You will have 12 strawberry-frosted cupcakes, which is 40% of the cupcakes you baked.

If you wanted to have 70% vanilla, on the other hand, you'd have the following:

$$\frac{70}{100} \times 30 = 21$$

21 of the cupcakes would have vanilla frosting, which is 70% of the cupcakes you baked.

# Ratios

A **ratio** shows the relationship between two different parts of a whole. Be careful not to confuse ratios with fractions, which compare one part to the whole. Here's what each looks like:

$$Fraction = \frac{part}{whole}$$

$$Ratio = \frac{part}{part}$$

A ratio can also be represented with a colon (:). Using our previous example, let's suppose you wanted to have a ratio of 3 cupcakes with vanilla frosting to 2 cupcakes with strawberry frosting. You could write the ratio as either $\frac{3}{2}$ or 3:2. This means that for every 3 vanilla-frosted cupcakes, there will be 2 strawberry-frosted ones.

If you were looking at the ratio of strawberry to vanilla cupcakes, however, you'd write it as $\frac{2}{3}$ or 2:3. There would still be 2 strawberry-frosted cupcakes for every 3 vanilla-frosted ones. You must always put the numbers in the same order as mentioned in the written-out version of the ratio.

# Proportions

Let's suppose that the bake sale you had earlier was a success and all the cupcakes were sold. You've decided to have another one, but this time you plan to bake 90 cupcakes instead of 30. You want to keep the same ratio of vanilla frosting to strawberry frosting, and you used vanilla frosting for 20 cupcakes during the first bake sale. How many vanilla-frosted cupcakes will you need this time?

You can use a **proportion** to figure this out. In a proportion, the relationship between parts or between a part and its whole stays the same. In order to figure out what the new number of cupcakes will be, you have to multiply each piece of the proportion by the same number.

For this problem, you know that 20 out of 30 total cupcakes had vanilla frosting and that you'll have 90 total cupcakes this time. You can set the proportion up like this:

$$\frac{20 \text{ vanilla}}{30 \text{ total}} = \frac{? \text{ vanilla}}{90 \text{ total}}$$

What do you multiply 30 by to get to 90? You multiply by 3. That means you should also multiply 20 by 3 too, which gives you 60.

$$\frac{20}{30} \begin{array}{c} \times 3 \\ \times 3 \end{array} = \frac{60}{90}$$

So, you'll need to frost 60 cupcakes with vanilla frosting. Make sure you have enough frosting!

You can use proportions to solve percent problems as well. Let's say you ran out of cupcake batter and only baked 50 cupcakes instead of 90. You decide to put strawberry frosting on 44% of the cupcakes. How many will have strawberry frosting?

Set up a proportion using the fraction form of the percent:

$$\frac{44}{100} = \frac{?}{50}$$

What do you multiply 100 by to get to 50? You multiply by .5 or $\frac{1}{2}$. That means you should multiply 44 by .5 too, which gives you 22.

$$\frac{44}{100} \begin{array}{c} \times .5 \\ \times .5 \end{array} = \frac{22}{50}$$

Always be sure to keep track of your numbers when setting up proportions—you have to put the same type of number on the top in both fractions. In the previous examples, we always put the number of frosted cupcakes that we were looking for on top and the total number of cupcakes baked on the bottom.

**ONE MORE THING...** Understanding percents and ratios helps us function in our world every day. Percents are used in stores, in surveys, and on nutrition labels, to name just a few examples. Not only do stores use percents to offer sales on certain items, but many states also charge a sales tax on most items—usually between 4% and 10% of the item's purchase price. Ratios are also used a lot. For instance, the ratio of students to teachers is used to advertise the amount of personal attention each student receives at a particular school.

# Participate

## Activity: Hands-On

**Survey time:** Survey your household or friends about their ice cream preferences. Count how many people prefer vanilla and how many prefer chocolate. Tally it up and report the ratio of the number of people who prefer vanilla to the number of people who prefer chocolate. Was it larger or smaller than you expected? Try the exercise again with different categories!

# In a Nutshell

**Definitions**

- **Percent:** a number divided by 100, such as 75% or $\frac{75}{100}$

- **Ratio:** a relationship between two parts, often written as $\frac{\text{part}}{\text{part}}$

**Rules**

- To set up a **proportion**, be sure to put the same thing on the top and bottom of each fraction:

$$\frac{5 \text{ apples}}{3 \text{ oranges}} = \frac{15 \text{ apples}}{9 \text{ oranges}}$$

# Mean, Median, and Mode

**P**ercent means "divided by 100." A **percent** tells you how much you have of something. **Mean**, **median**, and **mode** are three metrics that are used to describe groups of things. Each of these is a type of statistic. **Statistics** are what mathematicians use to interpret sets of data.

You will have to organize and analyze information many times in your life, including when you take various types of tests.

At the end of this lesson, you will be able to:

- understand the definitions of mean, median, and mode

- find mean, median, and mode

- solve word problems: translate words into math and math into words

**Parent's Corner**

One of the biggest challenges for sixth graders with mean, median, and mode is keeping the terms straight. Here's a good way to remember it. Mean = average, Median = middle, and Mode = most. Mean is the same concept as average; median is the middle number in an ordered set of numbers; and mode is the value that appears the *most* in a set.

# Dive Right In!

## Putting Statistics to Use

**Directions:** Three children packed for a trip. The items each child brought are listed in the following chart. Read the chart, and answer the questions below.

| Child | Shirts | Shoes (Pairs) | Hats | Pants (Pairs) |
|-------|--------|---------------|------|---------------|
| Mark | 3 | 2 | 4 | 1 |
| Susan | 6 | 3 | 1 | 2 |
| Thomas | 3 | 1 | 1 | 6 |

1. How many items did each child bring?

2. What is the mean number of shirts, pairs of shoes, hats, and pairs of pants brought?

3. What is the mode of the items brought? In other words, which item was brought most frequently?

4. What is the median number of shirts, pairs of shoes, hats, and pairs of pants brought?

5. What is the mean number of items brought by the children? Does this answer make sense?

*Answers can be found on page 188.*

# Explore

## Mean

The **mean** of a list of numbers is the average of all the numbers in the list. The mean is sometimes called the **arithmetic mean**. The mean can be either an integer or a decimal. Your math teacher figures out what your grade should be after six weeks of school by calculating the mean of all the grades you received during the six weeks.

You can find the mean of a list of numbers by adding up all the numbers in the list and dividing by the total amount of numbers in the list. That's all there is to it!

Look at the following list of numbers.

List A: {7, 5, 11, 16, 11, 10, 3}

Now let's find the mean.

First, add up all the numbers in the list.

$$7 + 5 + 11 + 16 + 11 + 10 + 3 = 63$$

Now, divide this total by the amount of numbers in the list. Because there are 7 numbers in the list, we divide 63 by 7 to get the mean: 9! Here's what the whole equation looks like.

$$\frac{7+5+11+16+11+10+3}{7} = 9$$

The mean of this list of numbers is 9.

## Median

The **median** of a list of numbers is the number in the middle of the list once you put the numbers in order from least (farthest left) to greatest (farthest right).

Let's find the median of the list of numbers we used above. This time we have to put the list of numbers in order from least to greatest before we can figure out the median.

List A: {3, 5, 7, 10, 11, 11, 16}

10 is the number in the middle of our list, so it is our median.

What if we had eight numbers in our list instead of seven? With an even number of numbers in the list, there's no one number in the middle. In this case, we can take the mean of the middle two numbers.

Let's add the number 8 to our list. Now we have an even number of numbers in the list. Once we put this list in order, we get the following:

List A: {3, 5, 7, 8, 10, 11, 11, 16}

8 and 10 are the middle two numbers in our list. To find the median, we calculate the mean of these two middle numbers.

$$\frac{8+10}{2} = 9$$

We know that the median of these eight numbers is 9. Whenever you see an even amount of numbers in your list (for example, four numbers or six numbers in a list), to find the median, you must remember to find the mean of the two middle numbers!

## Mode

The **mode** of a list of numbers is the number that appears most frequently in the list. Again, we can use our original set of seven numbers to find the mode.

List A: {7, 5, 11, 16, 11, 10, 3}

It is obvious that the number 11 appears more often than any of the others. Thus, 11 is our mode.

What if two or more numbers appear most frequently? Then we have more than one mode. What if no number in the list appears most frequently? Then there isn't a mode for that list of numbers.

## Translations

Sometimes you will have to translate words into math and vice versa. Consider the following sentence.

40 percent of 200 is what?

How can we do math with words? Well, we can't, but we can use the following chart to convert the words into mathematic symbols we can use.

| English | Math |
|---|---|
| what | ? |
| is, are, was | = |
| of | × |
| percent | $\dfrac{number}{100}$ |

Let's convert the following sentence into math:

40 percent of 200 is what?

*40 percent* converts to $\dfrac{40}{100}$.

*of* converts to "×" (or *multiplied by*).

200 stays as it is.

*is* converts to "=" (or *equals*).

After we've converted words into math, we get an arithmetic problem that is easy to solve because we know which operations to use to calculate the answer.

$$\frac{40}{100} \times 200 = ?$$

After we perform the arithmetic, we know that the answer is 80.

We can also go the other direction and translate math into words.

$$\frac{30}{100} \times 50 = ?$$

The math sentence above translates to: 30% of 50 is what? The answer is 15.

**ONE MORE THING...**

During your life, you will encounter many situations that will require you to organize numbers. If you work at a job involving money or you want to make a list of sports facts such as free throws per season or touchdown passes per game, you will need to know how to analyze numbers. How much money, on average, did your company earn over the past year? How does one player's batting average compare to another player's? These questions are some of the many that people ask themselves every day in order to better understand the patterns in the world around them.

# Participate

## Activity: Hands-On

Take a survey of the heights of your immediate family and, if possible, your extended family. Make a prediction of the mean (average) height of your family. Then calculate the mean, median, and mode (if there is a mode) of your family's heights. Did it match your prediction? How far off were you?

# In a Nutshell

**Definitions**

- **Mean**: the average of a set of numbers, sometimes called the arithmetic mean; it's found by adding up the numbers in a list and dividing by the amount of numbers in the list

- **Median**: the middle number in a list of numbers; when there are no numbers in the middle, then you take the average of the 2 numbers closest to the middle

- **Mode**: the most common number in a list; when no number is more common than another, there is no mode

**Answers for Dive Right In:**

1. Mark 10, Susan 12, Thomas 11

2. shirts 4, pairs of shoes 2, hats 2, pairs of pants 3

3. shirts

4. shirts 3, pairs of shoes 2, hats 1, pairs of pants 2

5. 2.75 items. No, we can't have two-thirds of an item!

# Order of Operations

In math, as in life, some things must be done in the correct order. For example, you can't get on the bus if you haven't yet left your home. Similarly, in math, operations must be done in the correct order, otherwise you will get the wrong result. In this chapter, you will learn the correct order of operations. You will also learn to write expressions using the correct order of operations to solve word problems.

At the end of this lesson, you will be able to:

- perform math operations in the correct order

- know the acronym PEMDAS and how to apply it to math problems

**Parent's Corner**

If you come across the expression $5(2)^2$, which do you do first? 5 times 2? Or 2 squared? The answer comes from the order of operations, PEMDAS. (Parentheses, Exponents, Multiplication, Division, Addition, Subtraction). Help your sixth grader remember the order of operations through "**P**lease **E**xcuse **M**y **D**ear **A**unt **S**ally" or any other mnemonic device you like!

# Dive Right In!

## *Expression Express*

**Directions:** With a partner, write a set of expressions as directed below. Then exchange your set of expressions with any two members of your household. Who can evaluate all the expressions first? Answers will vary.

### Expressions with One Operation

1.  Write an expression with addition and one or two negative integers.

2.  Write an expression with subtraction and one or two negative integers.

3.  Write an expression with multiplication and one or two negative integers.

4. Write an expression with addition and one or two mixed numbers.

· · · · · · · · · · · · · · · ●
**HINT**
*Questions 4–6: translate the mixed numbers to improper fractions BEFORE you add, subtract, multiply, or divide them!*

5. Write an expression with subtraction and one or two mixed numbers.

6. Write an expression with division and one or two mixed numbers.

## Expressions with More than One Operation

7. Write an expression with all four operations used at least once.

8. Write an expression with parentheses, an exponential expression, and at least two different operations.

# Explore

## Exponents

**Exponents** are a shorter way to write repeated multiplication. How could you show 2 used as a factor 3 times? (Remember, **factor** means a number that is multiplied.) You could write:

$$2 \times 2 \times 2$$

Or, you could write:

$$2^3$$

In the expression $2^3$, 2 is the **base**, and 3 is the **exponent**. When reading aloud $2^3$, say *two to the third power* or *two cubed*.

$$2^3 \longrightarrow \text{exponent}$$
$$\longrightarrow \text{base}$$

The base tells what number is being multiplied. The exponent tells how many times to use the base as a factor.

Be careful not to confuse an expression like $2^3$ (*two to the third power* or *two cubed*) with an expression like $3^2$ (*three to the second power* or *three squared*).

$$2^3 = 2 \times 2 \times 2 = 8$$

but

$$3^2 = 3 \times 3 = 9$$

and $8 \neq 9$

Now, try evaluating these examples:

$$3^2 \qquad\qquad\qquad 3^3$$

$$7^2 \qquad\qquad\qquad 7^3$$

$$10^2 \qquad\qquad\qquad 10^3$$

# PEMDAS

Now that you've learned about exponents, let's learn the order of operations. We'll use the order of operations to evaluate expressions with positive and negative numbers and with mixed numbers.

What does it mean to **evaluate an expression**? An expression is any combination of numbers, variables, and operations that does not include any equal signs or inequalities. These are examples of expressions:

$$5 + 3 \qquad 4^3 \qquad 7x \qquad (4 - 1)^2 \qquad 11y + 6 \qquad \frac{7}{9}$$

To evaluate an expression is to find the value of the expression. In other words, it is finding the number that the expression equals. When evaluating expressions, you need to use the correct order of operations.

First, do any operations inside **p**arentheses or other grouping symbols, such as brackets.

Next, evaluate any **e**xponential expressions.

Then, **m**ultiply and **d**ivide, *from left to right.*

Finally, **a**dd and **s**ubtract, *from left to right.*

Use the word **PEMDAS** to help you remember the order of operations:

**P**arentheses
**E**xponents
**M**ultiply
**D**ivide
**A**dd
**S**ubtract

If remembering the word PEMDAS is difficult, then use the sentence, "**P**lease **e**xcuse **m**y **d**ear Aunt Sally" to help you remember the order of operations.

Let's use the order of operations to evaluate the expression $7 + 2^3 \div (5 - 1) \times 9$.

| | | |
|---|---|---|
| $7 + 2^3 \div (5 - 1) \times 9$ | first... | Do the operations in parentheses. |
| $= 7 + 2^3 \div 4 \times 9$ | then... | Evaluate exponential expressions. |
| $= 7 + 8 \div 4 \times 9$ | then... | Multiply and divide, from left to right, by first dividing $8 \div 4 = 2$ and then multiplying $2 \times 9 = 18$. |
| $= 7 + 18$ | lastly... | Add. |
| $= 25$ | | |

Now let's consider this scenario: when given the problem $5 + 7 \times 2$, Ralph says the answer is 19, while Luisa says $5 + 7 \times 2 = 24$. Who is correct?

First, we see if there are any operations in parentheses. Because there are not, we then look for exponential expressions. Again, there are none. We then keep using PEDMAS to remind us of our next step.

| | | |
|---|---|---|
| $5 + 7 \times 2$ | then... | Multiply |
| $= 5 + 14$ | lastly... | Add |
| $= 19$ | | |

Thus, $5 + 7 \times 2 = 19$. Ralph was correct.

Now you try. Evaluate these expressions.

1.  $60 - 2(8 - 5)^3$

2.  $[4 + (50 \div 25)] \times 8$

3.  $52 - 6^2 + 40 \div (7 + 3) \times 2$

*Answers can be found on page 198.*

 **ONE MORE THING...** You will use the order of operations in every math course you take. Knowing the order of operations is as necessary as understanding what symbols like "×" and "÷" mean. Our common understanding of both these symbols and the order of operations is part of what makes communication in math possible.

You use steps for solving problems outside of math classes too. For any problem you have, you first figure out what the problem is, come up with a way to solve it, follow through on your plan, and then check that your actions actually solved the problem.

# Participate

## *Activity: Hands-On*

Make an index card with the steps of PEMDAS and quiz yourself and your partner or sibling. Now that you are an expert in PEMDAS and the Order of Operations, try to stump your partner by creating a tricky math expression that requires your partner to use all of the steps!

Example: $\dfrac{18}{3} - 7 + 2 \times 5$

# In a Nutshell

## Definitions

- **Exponent:** a shorter way to write repeated multiplication; the base tells what number to multiply, and the exponent tells how many times to use the base as a factor
- **Factor:** a number that is multiplied
- **Expression:** any combination of numbers, variables, and operations that does not include an equals sign or inequality sign
- **Evaluate:** to find the value of; to evaluate an expression is to calculate what number it equals
- **PEMDAS:** a way to remember the order of operations: Parentheses, Exponents, Multiply and Divide, Add and Subtract

## Rules

- **The Order of Operations:** First, do any operations inside parentheses or other grouping symbols, such as brackets. Next, evaluate any exponential expressions. Then, multiply and divide, from left to right. Finally, add and subtract, from left to right.

**Answers for Explore: Exponents:**

$3^2 = 9$, $3^3 = 27$

$7^2 = 49$, $7^3 = 343$

$10^2 = 100$, $10^3 = 1000$

 **Answers for Explore: PEMDAS:**

1. $60 - 2(8 - 5)^3 = 6$
2. $[4 + (50 \div 25)] \times 8 = 48$
3. $52 - 6^2 + 40 \div (7 + 3) \times 2 = 24$

# Factoring

We set different types of goals every day, from saving money for something special, to getting good grades, to becoming better at a certain sport or activity. Sometimes achieving your goal can seem overwhelming if you only think about the end result. When you work toward a goal, it helps to break the big job into a bunch of smaller jobs so the work seems a bit easier.

Being able to break a complex problem down into a simpler one is a useful skill in math. Factoring breaks a number down into smaller numbers that are easier to work with.

At the end of this lesson, you will be able to:

- create factor trees to identify the prime factors of a number

- identify the greatest common factor for given numbers

**Parent's Corner**

Remind your sixth grader of the difference between *factors* and *multiples*. E.g. 3 is a factor of 9 because it goes into 9 evenly, whereas 18 is a multiple of 9 because 9 times 2 is 18. Additionally, quiz your sixth grader on what makes a prime number a prime number. (Prime numbers are special: they are numbers that have only two factors: themselves and 1; the smallest prime number is 2.) Can they name some prime numbers, like 2, 3, 5, 7? Help your student visualize breaking up larger numbers into their *prime factors* by drawing factor trees and hanging them up.

# Dive Right In!

## *Factor Relay*

**Directions:** For this activity, you have to answer each question to know what to do on the next question. Start with the first question at the top of the chart. When you have answered the first question, record your answer next to letter (A). Use that number to replace the letter (A) in the next question in order to understand what you are supposed to do. Keep replacing the letters in the questions with your number answer from the previous question until you get to the end. Read carefully! Making a mistake early on will prevent you from getting the correct final answer.

| | |
|---|---|
| What is the sum of the 7 smallest positive integers? | (A) |
| How many factors of (A) are there? | (B) |
| What is the smallest prime factor of (B)? | (C) |
| What is the product of the next (C) integers greater than 5? | (D) |
| What is the sum of all of the prime factors of (D)? | (E) |
| How many pairs of factors does (E) have? | (F) |
| What is the sum of the next (F) integers greater than 10? | (G) |
| What is the greatest common factor of (G) and 40? | (H) |

| | |
|---|---|
| What is the sum of the first (H) positive even integers? | (I) |
| What is the largest prime factor of (I)? | (J) |
| What is the product of (J) and the only even prime number? | (K) |
| How many factors does (K) have? | (L) |
| What is the sum of the next (L) integers greater than 9? | (M) |
| What is the sum of all the prime factors of (M)? | (N) |
| What is the greatest common factor of (N) and 10? | Final Answer: |

*Answers can be found on page 210.*

# Explore

## Factors: The Basics

**Factors** are all the numbers that divide evenly into a particular number. For example, 2 is a factor of 8 because it goes in exactly 4 times with nothing left over. 3 is *not* a factor of 8 because when you divide 8 by 3, you get a remainder: $8 \div 3 = 2.66$ or 2 remainder 2.

If two numbers multiplied together give you a certain number, then that certain number is divisible by the two numbers you multiplied together. For example:

$3 \times 5 = 15$, so 15 is divisible by 3 and 5.

**Factoring** (sometimes called **factorization**) is the process of listing all of the pairs of numbers you can multiply to get a certain number. For example, the factors of 12 are 1, 12, 2, 6, 3, and 4 because

$$1 \times 12 = 12$$

$$2 \times 6 = 12$$

$$3 \times 4 = 12$$

When you are asked to find the factors of a number, write your factors in pairs so you don't leave any out.

The factors of 18 are

1 and _____

2 and _____

3 and _____

Is 4 a factor of 18? _____ Why? _____

Find the factors of the following numbers:

|         |         |          |
|---------|---------|----------|
| 32      | 49      | 100      |

*Answers can be found on page 210.*

Knowing some rules of divisibility can save you some time when finding the factors of a number.

| A number is divisible by... | If... |
|---|---|
| 2 | It is even. |
| 3 | The sum of all the digits in the number is divisible by 3. |
| 4 | The last 2 digits are divisible by 4. |
| 5 | It ends in 5 or 0. |
| 6 | It is divisible by 2 and 3. |
| 9 | The sum of all the digits in the number is divisible by 9. |
| 10 | It ends in 0. |

# Prime Factors and Factor Trees

**Prime factors** are the smallest integers into which a larger number can be broken. Remember that a prime number is only divisible by itself and 1.

To find the prime factors of a number, make a **factor tree.** Keep all the prime numbers on the left "branches." Start with the smallest prime number that you can (remember that 1 is *not* prime!). Once you have broken everything on the tree into prime numbers, you multiply all of the prime numbers together to show the **prime factorization.**

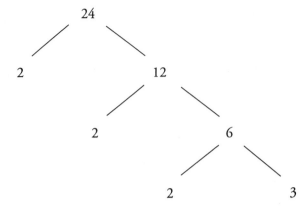

The prime factorization of 24 is 2 × 2 × 2 × 3.

2 is the smallest prime factor of 24, but 3 is also a prime factor of 24. What if we had started with 3 on the first branch instead of 2? Our tree would look like this:

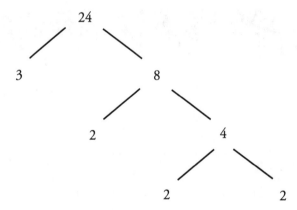

Notice that we get the same prime factors, just in a different order:
3 × 2 × 2 × 2.

You can see that as long as you break every number down by placing prime numbers on the left of each tree branch, it will be easy to see the prime factorization. It also helps to start your factor tree with the smallest prime number and its factor pair.

Make your own factor trees to find the prime factorization of the following numbers:

45                         36                         33

Prime numbers are the basic building blocks of math. Thinking of numbers in terms of their prime factors makes it easier to see connections between numbers, which can make multiplication and division easier.

For example, 9 × 16 might be difficult to calculate in your head.

However, we can break each of these numbers down into their prime factors:

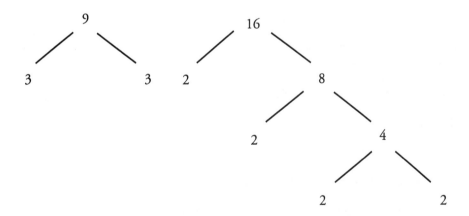

Now we can rewrite 9 × 16 as 3 × 3 × 2 × 2 × 2 × 2.

This can be rewritten as

$$3 \times 3 \times 4 \times 4 =$$

$$3 \times 4 \times 3 \times 4 =$$

$$12 \times 12 = 144$$

Prime factors can also help in reducing fractions because you can cancel out any numbers that are in both the numerator and denominator:

$$\frac{18}{42} = \frac{2 \times 3 \times 3}{2 \times 3 \times 7} = \frac{3}{7}$$

## Greatest Common Factor

When two or more numbers share a factor, that factor is called a **common factor**. In the fraction above, 2 and 3 are common factors of 18 and 42. When two numbers share the same prime factor, this is known at the **least common factor** (sometimes called the **LCF**).

The **greatest common factor** is the largest factor that two numbers have in common. You can find the greatest common factor (sometimes called the **GCF**) by multiplying all the prime common factors together.

Here's how you find the greatest common factor for 18 and 42:

18 $\longrightarrow$ ②  $\times$  ③  $\times$ 3

42 $\longrightarrow$ ②  $\times$  ③  $\times$ 7

18 and 42 have the prime factors 2 and 3 in common, so multiply 2 × 3 to find that 6 that is the greatest common factor.

This means that 6 is the largest number that can divide evenly into both 18 and 42.

Try the next examples.

1. The prime factors of 36 are _____

2. The prime factors of 45 are _____

3. What prime factors do 36 and 45 have in common? _____

4. Multiply the prime common factors together _____

5. The greatest common factor for 36 and 45 is _____

Finding the greatest common factor can save you some steps when reducing fractions.

If you want to reduce $\frac{24}{36}$, you have to divide the numerator and the denominator by the same number.

Both 24 and 36 are divisible by 2, so you can calculate $\dfrac{24 \div 2}{36 \div 2}$.

You are left with $\dfrac{12}{18}$, which can be reduced even further.

However, if you recognize that the greatest common factor for 24 and 36 is 12, you can reduce the fraction by dividing both numbers by 12. When you calculate $\dfrac{24 \div 12}{36 \div 12}$ you get $\dfrac{2}{3}$, which cannot be reduced any further.

## Helpful Tips for Factoring

- When you are asked to find the factors of a number, think about what numbers you can multiply together to get that number. Start with 1 and the number, and continue making your list in pairs so you don't leave any factors out.
- When you are asked to find the prime factors of a number, use a factor tree. Keep the prime factors on left branches, and keep breaking down the numbers on the right branches until you have all prime numbers.

**ONE MORE THING...** The ability to break down large numbers is a skill you can always rely on when the batteries in your calculator run out. You can use prime factoring to break down larger numbers to make multiplication and division easier. It's also helpful when you need to reduce fractions to their lowest terms.

 # Participate

## Activity: Hands-On

Find a deck of index cards and number them 10–50. Pick a card at random and on the other side of the card, use a factor tree to find the prime factorization of your number. Quiz your sibling or partner! Note that some numbers will be prime, and thus will only have two factors: 1 and itself.

# In a Nutshell

## Definitions

- **Factor:** a factor is a number that divides evenly into another number

- **Prime factor:** a factor that is also prime (divisible only by itself and 1). Prime factors are the smallest integers a number can be broken into.

- **Factoring:** making a list of all the factors for a number (sometimes called factorization)

- **Prime factorization:** breaking a number down into all of its prime factors

- **Common factor:** a factor that is shared by two or more numbers

- **Least common factor (LCF):** the smallest factor shared by two or more numbers

- **Greatest common factor (GCF):** the largest factor shared by two or more numbers

**Answers for Dive Right In:**

(A) 28 (1 + 2 + 3 + 4 + 5 + 6 + 7)

(B) 6 (1, 2, 4, 7, 14, 28)

(C) 2

(D) 42 (6 × 7)

(E) 12 (2 + 3 + 7)

(F) 3 (1 and 12, 2 and 6, 3 and 4)

(G) 36 (11 + 12 + 13)

(H) 4

(I) 20 (2 + 4 + 6 + 8)

(J) 5

(K) 10 (5 × 2)

(L) 4 (1, 2, 5, 10)

(M) 46 (10 + 11 + 12 + 13)

(N) 25 (2 + 23)

Final answer: 5

 **Answers for Explore: Factors the Basics:**

Factors of 18: 1 and 18, 2 and 9, 3 and 6; no, 4 is not a factor because it does not divide evenly into 18.

Factors of 32: 1, 2, 4, 8, 16, 32

Factors of 49: 1, 7, 49

Factors of 100: 1, 2, 4, 5, 10, 20, 25, 50, 100

 **Answers for Explore: Prime Factors:**

Prime factorization of 45: 3 × 3 × 5

Prime factorization of 36: 2 × 2 × 3 × 3

Prime factorization of 33: 3 × 11

 **Answers for Explore: Greatest Common Factor:**

1. Prime factors of 36: 2 × 2 × 3 × 3

2. Prime factors of 45: 3 × 3 × 5

3. Prime factors in common: 3 and 3

4. Multiply: 3 × 3

5. Greatest common factor of 36 and 45: 9

# Introduction to Algebra

Y ou already know algebra because you have been doing it since you learned to add, subtract, multiply, and divide. You just didn't know you were doing algebra!

At the end of this lesson, you will be able to:

- translate English expressions into an algebraic equation

- solve algebraic equations

**Parent's Corner**

For sixth graders, using variables as opposed to real numbers is a big step. They will use algebra for the rest of their math curriculum, so it is important to be clear about the fundamentals. If they are confused by $x$, $y$, or any letters used to represent a variable, help your student see that these symbols are not abstract, mysterious ideas; they actually represent *real numbers*.

# Dive Right In!

## *Got Your Nose*

**Directions:** The following two problems are about Samantha's business selling costumes to clowns. Translate both problems into algebra, and then solve the equations.

1. Samantha sold 12 clown noses during the day. At the end of the day she had 14 noses left. How many noses did Samantha have at the beginning of the day?

2. At the beginning of the day, Samantha had $12.00. At the end of the day, she had $38.00. How much money did she earn during the day?

*Answers can be found on page 218.*

# Explore

## Using Variables

Basic algebra is nothing more than taking a word problem and translating it into a math problem. Before you know what the answer is, you will assign a letter to represent what will eventually be the answer. We call this placeholder a **variable**. You can pick any letter as a variable. The most popular letter is $x$, but any letter will do.

Here's how this works.

1.  Before you leave for school, you have two books in your backpack. You realize that you will need three other books for school, and you put them into your backpack. Now how many books do you have in your backpack?

Let's transform this English sentence into an algebra equation. You begin with two books, so write down the number 2:

$$2$$

Next, you will put three more books into the backpack. This is adding books, so write down a plus sign and the number 3:

$$2 + 3$$

You are asked how many books are in the backpack, so you need to write an equals sign, and then you need to write a variable to take the place of the answer until we have finished solving the problem. You could pick $x$ or perhaps you might pick $b$ for books.

$$2 + 3 = b$$

You might have known that there were five books total, but now you know how to translate a word problem into algebra. You can see from the problem above that the variable $b$ equals 5, so the total number of books is also 5.

You will use this skill many times over the next few years, including on various test types!

# Solving Algebra Problems

As you just saw, you can solve word problems more easily by following these three steps:

- Translate the problem from English into a math equation.
- Do the calculations written in the math equation you just wrote.
- Use the answer you calculated to replace the variable.

You have just **solved for** $b$ (or whatever letter you choose)!

Let's try another problem, using algebra to solve it.

2. There are four people on a bus. At the first stop, three more people get on the bus. At the second stop, two people get off the bus, and one person gets on the bus. At the third stop, five people get off the bus. How many people remain on the bus?

First, let's translate the problem, one step at a time. We will use $p$ (for people) as our variable.

People on the bus at the beginning:

4

People on the bus after the first stop:

$4 + 3$

People on the bus after the second stop:

$4 + 3 - 2 + 1$

People on the bus after the third stop:

$4 + 3 - 2 + 1 - 5$

Final equation including the variable:

$4 + 3 - 2 + 1 - 5 = p$

Now that you have your equation, do the addition and subtraction on the left side of the equals sign:

$$1 = p$$

Now you have your answer. The variable $p$ stands for the number of people left on the bus. Because $p = 1$, there is 1 person left on the bus.

**ONE MORE THING...** Any time you need to solve mathematical calculations, you are using algebra. There is always a variable, although you may not have named it $x$ or $b$ or $p$ before today. You use algebra when you figure out how many weeks you must save money from mowing lawns in order to buy a comic book or how many games your team needs to win to make it into the playoffs. Use a variable any time you see words like "what" or "how many." When you see words like "is" or "are," you should write an equal sign. That's algebra!

# Participate

## Activity: Hands-On

Think of examples of using variables or unknowns (*x, y, z,* etc) in your everyday life and write a problem for your partner or sibling to solve. One example would be: If it is currently 11:30 A.M. and your soccer game begins at 3:30 P.M., how many *x*, the number of minutes remaining before the game?

# In a Nutshell

**Rules**

- Translate word problems into algebraic equations.

- Write down the numbers and operations needed to solve the problem.

- Write down an equal sign (=) in place of "is" or "are."

- Use a variable such as $x$ in place of "how many" or "what."

- Solve for the variable by performing the operations.

### Answers for Dive Right In:

Set up these equations, translating the word problems into math and using variables.

1. $12 + 14 = x$

   $26 = x$

   26 noses

2. $12 + x = 38$

   $26 = x$

   \$26

# Simplifying Expressions with Addition and Subtraction

**D**ifficult physical training isn't the only thing that can make you break a sweat. Sometimes big, long mathematical expressions or equations can give you quite a workout as well. But these expressions can be made much easier if you simplify them.

What does that mean? That means you add all the stuff together that's the same. To use a classic example, we're going to talk about apples and oranges. First, let's talk about only the apples. What if you had 4 apples and 6 apples? What do you get when you add them together?

Now let's say you've got 3 apples and 4 oranges. What do you get when you add them together?

At the end of this lesson, you will be able to:

- recognize similar terms
- combine like terms

---

**Parent's Corner**

The big lesson here is "combine like terms," which means that you should encourage your sixth grader to group like with like. Remember that variables ($x$, $y$, $z$, etc.) should be grouped with other variables, and numbers should be grouped with other numbers. It's as simple as that!

---

# Dive Right In!

## A Hairy Situation

**Directions:** Wayne works in a hair salon and needs to figure out how much money he can expect to make this week. To simplify this task, use what you have learned.

**Week's Appointments**

| Weekday | Time | Service Provided | Cost of Service |
|---------|------|------------------|-----------------|
| Monday | 9:00–10:00 | Permanent Wave | $100 |
| | 10:00–11:00 | Highlights | $150 |
| | 11:00–12:00 | Shampoo and Cut | $60 |
| | 12:00–1:00 | Shampoo and Cut | $60 |
| | Lunch | | |
| | 2:00–3:00 | Straightening | $600 |
| | 3:00–4:00 | | |
| | 4:00–5:00 | | |
| | 5:00–6:00 | | |

| Weekday | Time | Service Provided | Cost of Service |
|---|---|---|---|
| Tuesday | 9:00–10:00 | Children's Cut | $20 |
| | 10:00–11:00 | Highlights | $150 |
| | 11:00–12:00 | Highlights | $150 |
| | 12:00–1:00 | Shampoo and Cut | $60 |
| | Lunch | | |
| | 2:00–3:00 | Permanent Wave | $100 |
| | 3:00–4:00 | Highlights | $150 |
| | 4:00–5:00 | Shampoo and Cut | $60 |
| | 5:00–6:00 | Highlights | $150 |
| Wednesday | 9:00–10:00 | Straightening | $600 |
| | 10:00–11:00 | | |
| | 11:00–12:00 | | |
| | 12:00–1:00 | | |
| | Lunch | | |
| | 2:00–3:00 | Shampoo and Cut | $60 |
| | 3:00–4:00 | Shampoo and Cut | $60 |
| | 4:00–5:00 | Children's Cut | $20 |
| | 5:00–6:00 | Children's Cut | $20 |
| Thursday | 9:00–10:00 | Highlights | $150 |
| | 10:00–11:00 | Permanent Wave | $100 |
| | 11:00–12:00 | Shampoo and Cut | $60 |
| | 12:00–1:00 | Shampoo and Cut | $60 |
| | Lunch | | |
| | 2:00–3:00 | Permanent Wave | $100 |
| | 3:00–4:00 | Shampoo and Cut | $60 |
| | 4:00–5:00 | Highlights | $150 |
| | 5:00–6:00 | Shampoo and Cut | $60 |

| Weekday | Time | Service Provided | Cost of Service |
| --- | --- | --- | --- |
| Friday | 9:00–10:00 | Straightening | $600 |
| | 10:00–11:00 | | |
| | 11:00–12:00 | | |
| | 12:00–1:00 | | |
| | Lunch | | |
| | 2:00–3:00 | Permanent Wave | $100 |
| | 3:00–4:00 | Children's Cut | $20 |
| | 4:00–5:00 | Going home early! | Going home early! |
| | 5:00–6:00 | | |

Gather all of the different services together and make an equation out of them. How much money will Wayne bring in this week?

*Answers can be found on page 229.*

# **Explore**

## Combining Like Terms

We're not here to talk about fruit, but the fruit analogy on page 219 can help us with math. Take a look at this expression.

⇨    $18x^2 + 24y + 2x + 4x^2 + 2y + 8x =$

We can **combine like terms** (the things that are the same) to simplify the expression. Like terms can be added or subtracted, depending on the sign in front of them, to simplify. In order for terms to be *like* terms, they need to share the same kind of variable. Pair an $x$ with an $x$, an $x^2$ with an $x^2$, and so on. What are the like terms in this equation? A good way to start when you're looking for like terms is to start with the first term, in this case $18x^2$.

1.    What else looks like $18x^2$? Write all the terms that do here.

2.    What do we do with these terms? Add? Subtract? Multiply? Divide? How do you know?

3.    What is the next set of like terms? List them here.

4.    What do we do with these terms? How do you know?

5.  What is another set of like terms in this equation?

6.  What do we do with these terms?

7.  Now combine everything we've simplified into one equation.

That's how we simplify equations!

*Answers can be found on page 229.*

> ## Helpful Hint
> When combining like terms, look at the exponent and variables in a term. You can only combine like exponents and variables.

## Combining Constants

Combining like terms also works with **constants** (numbers that aren't variables) in the same way. Simplify this example.

➡  $18y^3 + 14 + 2y^2 + 4y^3 + 27 =$

1.  First, is anything similar to the first term? Combine all the terms like the first term.

2.  What's the next term to combine? Combine all the terms like this one.

3. Do the same for all other like terms here.

4. If there are no more like terms, you've simplified as much as you can. Combine everything to get a complete, simplified expression and you're done!

Try one more from start to finish!

⇨ $40y^2 + 20y - 31 - 35y^2 + 29 - 19y =$

*Answers can be found on page 229.*

## Simplifying Equations

You can simplify on both sides of the equals sign. When you combine two terms on different sides of the equals sign, you "undo" the operation.

⇨ $16p + 40 - 5p^2 + 14p = 60 - 5p^2 =$

1. First, combine all the terms like the first term. Both of these terms are on the same side of the equals sign.

2. Now, when you combine all the terms like the next term, you see that one term is on the other side of the equal sign, so you "undo" the operation in front of it to bring it over to the other side. Essentially, you subtract 40 from both sides of the equation. You must always do the same thing to both sides of the equal sign.

3.  Combine all the terms like the next term.

4.  Combine everything to get a simplified expression.

5.  This equation can be manipulated so you have variables on one side and constants on the other. Manipulate it here.

6.  Now you can solve for $p$.

*Answers can be found on page 229.*

**ONE MORE THING...** When you simplify in math, just like everything else in life, things get easier. You boil a big problem down to its basic form. Sometimes you can solve for the variable, sometimes you have a much easier version of the expression or equation to work with. Either way, it makes math easier and can save you time. A win-win!

# Participate

## Activity: Hands-On

Look around your kitchen for some nuts or other small objects that can be counted and sorted as "like terms." For instance, you might label the peanuts as *x* and count them (maybe you have 40 peanuts, so "40*x*"); and you might label the pistachios as *y* and count them as well (maybe you have 12 pistachios, so "12*y*.") You're combining like terms! This could also be done with different types of coins. Ask your parents for some spare change and find out how many pennies (*p*), nickels (*n*), dimes (*d*), and quarters (*q*) you have.

# In a Nutshell

**Definitions**

- **Terms:** parts of an equation that can be added to or subtracted from each other
- **Combining Like Terms:** adding all of the similar terms in an equation into one term
- **Constants:** regular numbers that can be thought of as terms

**Answers for Dive Right In:**

Create variables for each of the services. It helps to clarify these with the class up front, since a few different services could have the same letter. For instance,

Permanent Wave could be $p$

Highlights could be $h$

Shampoo and Cut could be $o$

Straightening could be $s$

Children's Cut could be $c$

The final expression should look something like $4c + 7h + 10o + 5p + 3s$

Replacing the variables with the price of the service makes it possible to find the amount of money earned:

$4(\$20) + 7(\$150) + 10(\$60) + 5(\$100) + 3(\$600) = \$4,030.$

 **Answers for Explore: Combining Like Terms:**

1. $4x^2$

2. Add unless a term has a negative sign, which indicates subtraction

3. $24y$ and $2y$

4. Add, because there is no negative sign in the terms

5. $2x$ and $8x$

6. Add

7. $22x^2 + 10x + 26y$ (in the final, simplified expression terms are arranged alphabetically and from highest exponent to lowest.)

 **Answers for Explore: Combining Constants:**

1. $18y^3 + 4y^3 = 22y^3$

2. constants: $14 + 17 = 41$

3. $2y^2$ has no like terms

4. $22y^3 + 2y^2 + 41$

Arrow: $5y^2 + y - 2$

 **Answers for Explore: Simplifying Equations:**

1. $16p + 14p = 30p$

2. $60 - 40 = 20$

3. $-5p^2 + 5p^2 = 0$

4. $30p = 20$ (If 60 subtracted, $30p - 20 = 0$)

5. $30p = 20$

6. $p = \dfrac{20}{30} = \dfrac{2}{3}$

# Solving Equations

Let's say you have $100 in your pocket and you want to buy 10 items in your favorite store, and the total cost of these items was $100. You would be able to buy all 10 items. Why? The total value of the 10 items is equal to the value of the money you have. An **equation** is simply a way of stating that two amounts are equal.

Equations sometimes have an unknown value. A **variable** is an unknown quantity within the equation. Often, a symbol such as $x$ or $y$ or $a$ is used to show the variable. An equation with a variable looks a lot like this:

$$2x^2 = 9 + x^2$$

At the end of this lesson, you will be able to:

- balance equations

- solve an equation with a variable

**Parent's Corner**

If there's one thing you remember from algebra, it's probably *balancing equations*, right? Here is your chance to show off your balancing skills to your sixth grader. They will follow your example! Just keep reiterating the rule: what we do to one side of the equation, we *must* do to the other side.

# Dive Right In!

## *Shh!*

**Directions:** Write an equation on a piece of paper. Exchange it with a partner. Solve each other's equations. Answers will vary.

# Explore

## Equations

Think of an equation as a seesaw or teeter-totter. If a heavier adult is on one side of the seesaw and a lighter child is on the other, what happens? The side the adult is on quickly drops to the ground, and the side with the child goes up in the air.

To balance an equation, you need to put the same amount on each side, just as you would on a seesaw. The equal sign in the center of the equation indicates that both sides have the same amount or value. Let's look at a couple of equations that are balanced correctly.

$$10 + 20 = 30$$

$$5 - 3 = 2$$

$$2 \times 4 = 8$$

$$5 = 10 \div 2$$

Each of these equations has the same value on each side of the equal sign.

What would happen if you wanted to take away or add a certain amount to just one side of an equation? How would you keep the seesaw balanced?

# Balancing Equations

If you take away or add a certain amount to one side of an equation, the seesaw will tip to one side. In order to keep it balanced, you must take away or add the same amount to the other side. This is known as **balancing an equation**.

Let's look again at the four equations we saw earlier.

$$10 + 20 = 30$$
$$5 - 3 = 2$$
$$2 \times 4 = 8$$
$$5 = 10 \div 2$$

If you decide to take 10 away from the left side of the equation $10 + 20 = 30$, you will need to take 10 away from the right side of the equation to keep it balanced.

$$10 + 20 - 10 = 30 - 10$$

You will now have 20 on the left side and 20 on the right side of the equal sign. Your equation is still balanced!

Likewise, if you decide to add 4 to the left side of the equation $5 - 3 = 2$, you will need to add 4 to the right side of the equation to keep it balanced.

$$5 - 3 + 4 = 2 + 4$$

You will now have 6 on the left side and 6 on the right side of the equal sign. Again, your equation is still balanced!

Now you try it.

1. Divide both sides of the equation $2 \times 4 = 8$ by 2. What do you end up with on each side? Show your work.

2. Multiply both sides of the equation $5 = 10 \div 2$ by 5. What do you end up with on each side? Show your work.

## Solving Equations with Variables

As you read earlier, a variable is simply a symbol that represents an unknown value in an equation. Let's put variables in the four equations we've been using.

$$10 + 20 - x = 30$$

$$5 - 3 + a = 2$$

$$2 \times 4 \div b = 8$$

$$5 = 10 \div 2 \times t$$

To solve an equation with a variable, you will need to **isolate the variable**. Isolating the variable is just a fancy way of saying, "Get the variable all by itself on one side of the equation."

To isolate the variable, follow the rules of balancing an equation. For example, let's solve the following equation by isolating the variable.

3.    Let's find $x$ in $17 + x = 20$. What might be a useful first step?

We want to get the $x$ by itself. So, let's subtract 17 from the left side of the equation.

Remember, we need to keep the equation balanced. So, what is the second step?

You must subtract 17 from the right side of the equation in order to keep it balanced.

To review, you took 17 away from the left side of the equation in order to isolate the variable. However, to keep the equation balanced, you also had to take 17 from the right side of the equation.

What does your equation look like now?

So, what does this new equation tell you? It tells you that the variable, $x$, is equal to 3. You have just solved for the variable, or found its value.

Let's try another one. Solve the following equation by isolating the variable.

4. $2x \div 5 = 30$. This one looks a bit different, but the rules are the same. What is the first step?

We want to get the $x$ by itself, but we need to follow the order of operations as well. Because we are now dealing with division and multiplication, we must use those operations to isolate the variable. So, let's multiply the left side of the equation by 5.

Are we done? No, we need to also multiply the right side of the equation by 5. Now what does the equation look like? Write out your work here:

Your equation should now look like this: $2x = 150$.

We are still not done, because we have not solved the equation by isolating the variable yet. What is the next step?

In order to get the $x$ all by itself, we need to find a way to get rid of the 2. Because the 2 is being multiplied by $x$, let's divide the left side by 2. Of course, we will have to do the same thing to the right side of the equation.

You have now isolated the variable and solved for the unknown. If everything came out right, you will see that $x$ is equal to 75.

*Answers can be found on page 240.*

 ONE MORE THING... You've been solving equations for a long time. You see them everywhere! For example, let's say you go to the store to buy 10 pencils. The display sign may say 2 pencils cost 10 cents. How will you figure out how much 10 pencils will cost? You will probably set up the equation (2 pencils)(10 cents) = (10 pencils)($x$ cents) and solve it in your head without even realizing it.

Lots of careers require people to solve equations that are much more complicated than the ones we've talked about today. Bankers, scientists, and architects are just a few of the people who work with tough equations every day.

# Participate

## *Activity: Hands-On*

Grab some index cards! With a partner, play "Equation Concentration." Write equations such as $y + 6 = 20$ on one set of cards. Write solutions on another set of card. Remember, $y$ can be any number.

Spread out the equation cards on the left side and the solution cards on the right. Each player takes turns picking up an equation card and a solution card to make matches. The player with the most matches wins the game.

# In a Nutshell

## Definitions

- **Equation:** a way of showing that 2 amounts are equal; it always has an equal sign

- **Variable:** an unknown quantity in an equation; it is usually shown with a lowercase letter, such as $x$

- **Balancing an Equation:** what you do to one side of an equation must be done to another side of the equation

- **Isolating the Variable:** balancing the equation so that a variable is alone on one side, also known as solving an equation

## Hints

- What you do to one side of an equation you must do to the other.

- Remember to use PEMDAS.

**Answers for Explore: Balancing Equations:**

    1. $4 = 4$

    2. $5(5) = 5(10 \div 2); 25 = 25$

 **Answers for Explore: Solving Equations with Variables:**

    3. Subtract 17 from both sides, so that you can solve for $x$.

    4. Multiply each side by 5.

# Algebra and Order of Operations

**R**ead the following sentence:

*I'm reading a very good student's essay.*

There are two ways to interpret the sentence: either the essay is very good, or the student is very good. In literature, in fact, authors often intend for their work to have multiple interpretations. But math is built upon consistency. If $2 + 2 = 4$ today, then $2 + 2 = 4$ tomorrow.

But what about $7 - 3 \times 2$? Which operation should we do first? Should we do the subtraction first?

$$7 - 3 \times 2 \qquad\qquad 4 \times 2 = 8$$

Or should we do the multiplication first?

$$7 - 3 \times 2 \qquad\qquad 7 - 6 = 1$$

Is 8 the right answer, or is 1? There is a way to find the value of this expression and get the same value every time—**PEMDAS**!

At the end of this lesson, you will be able to:

- use PEMDAS to evaluate expressions

- use inverse operations to solve algebraic equations

---

**Parent's Corner**

Remind your sixth grader that there is a method to the madness. Our ultimate goal is to isolate the variable, of course, but getting there often requires two steps: (1) Add or subtract to get the variable and its coefficient (i.e., the 3 in "$3x$") on one side and a number on the other. (2) Multiply or divide both sides to get rid of the coefficient. Often, sixth graders will want to immediately divide both sides of the equation by the coefficient, but nudge them to do the first step first. Add or subtract, and *then* divide to multiply.

---

# Dive Right In!

## Sending a Package

**Directions:** The post office and other companies that ship packages use formulas, including linear equations, to figure out how much to charge you for a shipment. Read the directions below, and answer the following questions.

At Ship-It, the cost to ship packages is given by the following formula:

$$p = 0.8 + 0.2w$$

In this equation, $p$ is the price, in dollars, to ship the package, and $w$ is the weight of the package, in ounces (16 ounces = 1 pound). How much would it cost to ship a package that weighs 2 pounds? First, find how many ounces are in 2 pounds: 2 pounds × 16 ounces per pound = 32 ounces. Now, let's use the formula.

| $p = 0.8 + 0.2w$ | Start with the formula. |
|---|---|
| $p = 0.8 + 0.2 \times 32$ | Plug the number of ounces into the formula: $w = 32$. |
| $p = 0.8 + 6.4$ | Use PEMDAS and multiply first: $0.2 \times 32 = 6.4$. |
| $p = 7.2$ | Use PEMDAS and now add: $0.8 + 6.4 = 7.2$. |

So it would cost $7.20 to ship a package that weighs 2 pounds.

We can use this formula to find the cost to ship any package at Ship-It. Just plug the weight of the package, in ounces, into the formula, and then solve.

1. It would cost _____ to ship a 1-ounce package.

2. It would cost _____ to ship a 10-ounce package.

3. It would cost _____ to ship a 1-pound package.

4. It would cost _____ to ship a 5-pound package.

Ship-It delivers a package to you. You see that it cost $5.60 to ship the package. You're curious how much the package weighs. You can use the formula to find out, but now we'll plug in 5.60 for $p$, and solve for $w$.

| | |
|---|---|
| $p = 0.8 + 0.2w$ | Start with the formula. |
| $5.60 = 0.8 + 0.2w$ | Plug the cost, in dollars, into the formula: $p = 5.60$. |
| $4.8 = 0.2w$ | Subtract 0.8 from both sides: $5.6 - 0.8 = 4.8$. |
| $24 = w$ | Divide both sides by 0.2: $4.8 \div 0.2 = 24$. |

So, the package weighs 24 ounces, which is the same as one and a half pounds ($24 \div 16 = 1.5$).

5. A package that costs $2.40 must weigh _____ ounces.

6. A package that costs $23.20 must weigh _____ ounces, which is the same as _____ pounds.

7. A package that costs $32.80 must weigh _____ ounces, which is the same as _____ pounds.

Ship-It also has a flat-rate box that costs $13.00. You can use this box to ship any package weighing between 1 and 5 pounds. For some packages, it will be cheaper to use the normal rate. For other packages, it will be cheaper to use the flat rate.

8.  The flat-rate price and the normal price are the same when a package weighs _____ ounces.

9.  The cheapest way to send a package that weighs 4 pounds would be the _____ rate.

*Answers can be found on page 256.*

 # Explore

## More PEMDAS

PEMDAS is a word you can use to remember the **order of operations**. The order of operations tells us the sequence in which we should do the operations in an expression: **P**arentheses, **E**xponents, **M**ultiplication & **D**ivision, and then **A**ddition & **S**ubtraction, or PEMDAS. The sentence "**P**lease **E**xcuse **M**y **D**ear **A**unt **S**ally" can help you remember PEMDAS, and the following diagram can help you remember how to use it:

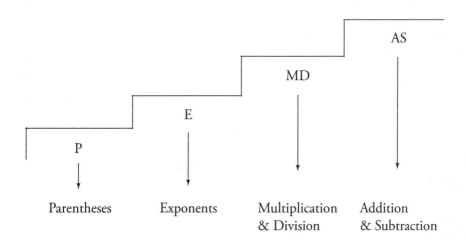

With each step on the staircase, we'll do the operations from left to right (just as we read a sentence). For instance, when we get to the Multiplication & Division step, we will search through the expression and do any multiplication or division, from left to right, until there isn't any multiplication or division left to do.

The first step is **Parentheses**. Before we do any other operations, we will do any operations inside parentheses or any other grouping symbols.

| $5 - (3 + 2) = 5 - 5$ | Do the operation inside the parentheses first. $3 + 2 = 5$. |
|---|---|
| $= 0$ | |

We may even see square brackets or curly brackets inside of parentheses. These grouping symbols work just like parentheses. We will just do the operations from the inside out.

| | |
|---|---|
| $7 \times (5 - [4 \div \{3 + 1\}]) = 7 \times (5 - [4 \div 4])$ | Do the operation inside the most grouping symbols first: $3 + 1 = 4$. |
| $= 7 \times (5 - 1)$ | Do the operations inside two grouping symbols next: $4 \div 4 = 1$. |
| $= 7 \times 4$ | Do the operation inside the parentheses next: $5 - 1 = 4$. |
| $= 28$ | |

The next step is the **Exponents**. Remember, exponents tell us how many of a certain number we should multiply together. For instance, $4^3 = 4 \times 4 \times 4$, because the exponent, 3, tells us to multiply three 4s together.

| | |
|---|---|
| $5 + 2^2 = 5 + (2 \times 2)$ | The expression includes no parentheses, so start with the exponent. |
| $= 5 + 4$ | |
| $= 9$ | |

The step after that is **Multiplication & Division**. Do multiplication and division from left to right.

| | |
|---|---|
| $20 - 6 \div 2 \times 5 = 20 - 3 \times 5$ | The expression includes no parentheses or exponents, so start by doing multiplication and division from left to right: $6 \div 2 = 3$. |
| $= 20 - 15$ | Do the multiplication next: $3 \times 5 = 15$. |
| $= 5$ | |

Remember, both "×" and "•" are used to show multiplication. There is another way of showing multiplication that you will often see in algebra. This way of showing multiplication uses parentheses. Consider this expression.

| | |
|---|---|
| $4 + 3(9 - 7) = 4 + 3(2)$ | Start by doing the operation in parentheses: $9 - 7 = 2$. |
| $= 4 + 6$ | $3(2)$ means $3 \times 2$, and $3 \times 2 = 6$. |
| $= 10$ | |

In an expression like $3(9 - 7)$, everything inside the parentheses is multiplied by 3. But you do the operation inside the parentheses first, as part of the Parentheses step, and get $3(2)$, then multiply as part of the Multiplication & Division step.

Last, we have the final step, **Addition & Subtraction**. Again, we do these operations from left to right.

| | |
|---|---|
| $5 - 1 + 2 = 4 + 2$ | The expression includes no parentheses, exponents, multiplication, or division, so just do addition and subtraction from left to right: $5 - 1 = 4$. |
| $= 6$ | |

You can use PEMDAS to evaluate very long and complicated expressions. Just do it one step at a time, looking for any parentheses in the expression, then looking for any exponents, then doing multiplication and division from left to right, and finally doing addition and subtraction from left to right.

Evaluate this expression. After you do each operation, rewrite the entire expression underneath the old one. We've done the first step for you.

$$6 \div 3 + (5 - 1) \times 3 + (6 \times [4 - 1]) \div 9 = 6 \div 3 + (5 - 1) \times 3 + (6 \times 3) \div 9$$

*Answers can be found on page 256.*

The order of operations is very important when we are solving algebraic equations. Next, we'll learn how to solve 1-step algebraic equations.

# Inverse Operations

Let's say someone gives you directions to a store that is near your house.

The directions are

1. Face right.
2. Walk 3 blocks.
3. Turn left.
4. Walk 2 blocks.

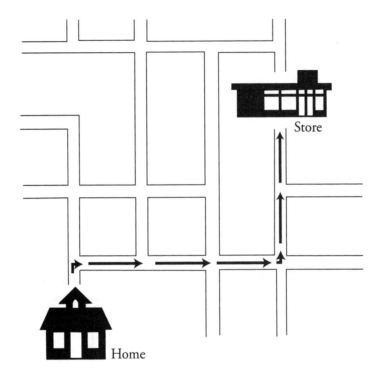

Now you want to go from the store back to your house. But we can't follow the directions we have in the same order we used to get to the store. If we start out from the store, face right, and try to walk 3 blocks, we see there's no road! Instead, we're going to have to follow our original directions backwards, undoing each step.

The opposite of the original directions are

1. Walk 2 blocks.
2. Turn right.
3. Walk 3 blocks.
4. Face left.

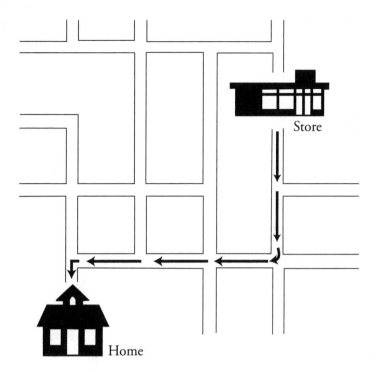

To solve equations, we do the exact same thing: work backwards. To solve an equation means to find the value of a **variable**, such as $x$, in an equation. The variable stands for an unknown number. To find the value of that unknown number, we need to work backwards, "undoing" each operation, until $x$ is all by itself on one side of the equation. We use **inverse operations** to undo each operation. Addition and subtraction are inverse operations. Multiplication and division are inverse operations.

Look at the following equation:

$$x + 3 = 11$$

Our goal is to get the $x$ all by itself on one side of the equal sign. Let's get rid of the + 3. What's the opposite of adding 3? Subtracting 3, because addition and subtraction are inverse operations.

The equal sign in an equation means that the expressions on either side have the same value. To keep both sides of the equation equal, anything you do to one side of an equation must also be done to the other side of the equation.

For example, take a look at the following equation.

$$8 = 8$$

Looks good, right? Well, you can add 4 to both sides and it's still a true statement.

$$8 + 4 = 8 + 4$$

$$12 = 12$$

You can also multiply both sides by the same number, and the equation is still true.

$$8 = 8$$

$$8 \times 2 = 8 \times 2$$

$$16 = 16$$

But what if you try adding to just one side of the equation?

$$8 = 8$$

$$8 = 8 + 1$$

$$8 = 9$$

We ended up with something that we know is not true: $8 \neq 9$. We can't add, subtract, multiply, or divide just one side of the equation: we have to do the same operations on both sides of an equation. Otherwise, we lose the "equal" part of the *equa*tion.

This is one of the most important rules in algebra: any operation done to one side of an equation must also be done to the other side.

Therefore, we can't subtract 3 from just one side, we have to subtract 3 from both sides of the equation.

$$
\begin{array}{ccccc}
x & + & 3 & = & 11 \\
  &   & -3 &   & -3 \\
\hline
x & + & 0 & = & 8 \\
  &   & x & = & 8
\end{array}
$$

Let's do another one.

$$2x = 24$$

In this equation, 2 is a **coefficient**. A coefficient is a number that is multiplied by a variable or variables. In other words, $2x$ is just another way to write $2 \cdot x$.

This equation tells us that two times $x$ is 24. To solve for $x$, we need to get rid of that 2. What is the opposite of multiplying by 2? Dividing by 2. Remember, multiplication and division are inverse operations. Each undoes the other.

| $2x = 24$ | Divide both sides by 2. |
|---|---|
| $\dfrac{2x}{2} = \dfrac{24}{2}$ | |
| $x = 12$ | |

## Two-Step Equations

Remember, if we are solving for a **variable** such as $x$ in an equation, then we need to "undo" each operation in the equation until $x$ is all by itself on one side of the equation. We use **inverse operations** to undo each operation. Addition and subtraction are inverse operations. Multiplication and division are also inverse operations.

Think of solving an equation as unwrapping a present with a ribbon around it. When the present was wrapped, it was covered in wrapping paper first, and then the ribbon was tied around it. To unwrap the present, you work in the opposite order, first undoing the ribbon, and then ripping off the wrapping paper.

We solve for $x$ in an equation in the same way: by using PEMDAS backwards. We start by undoing any addition and subtraction, and then we undo any multiplication and division.

Take a look at the following equation:

$$4x + 6 = 30$$

Our goal is to get the $x$ all by itself on one side of the equal sign. Let's get rid of the + 6 first. What's the opposite of adding 6? Subtracting 6, because addition and subtraction are inverse operations.

In an equation, the expressions on either side of the equal sign must stay equal. Therefore, anything you do to one side of an equation must also be done to the other side of the equation. This is one of the most important rules in algebra: any operation done to one side of an equation must also be done to the other side. We can't repeat this enough!

So we can't just subtract 6 from one side of the equation above. We have to subtract 6 from both sides of the equation.

$$
\begin{array}{rccc}
4x & + & 6 & = & 30 \\
& & -6 & & -6 \\
\hline
4x & + & 0 & = & 24 \\
& & 4x & = & 24
\end{array}
$$

So, now the equation is $4x = 24$. In this equation, 4 is a **coefficient**. A coefficient is a number that a variable or variables are multiplied by. What's the opposite of multiplying by 4? Dividing by 4. Multiplication and division are inverse operations: One undoes the other.

$$4x = 24$$

$$\frac{4x}{4} = \frac{24}{4}$$

$$x = 6$$

Now, take a look at this equation.

$$\frac{x}{4} - 7 = 13$$

We can think of the $x$ in this equation as having a coefficient of $\frac{1}{4}$. We can also think of the $x$ as being divided by 4. Both ways of thinking are correct. We solve this equation in the same way as the previous one: we use inverse operations. First, we add to get rid of the subtraction. Then, we multiply to get rid of the division.

$$
\begin{array}{rcccl}
\dfrac{x}{4} & - & 7 & = & 13 \qquad \text{Add 7 to both sides.} \\
& + & 7 & & +7 \\
\hline
\dfrac{x}{4} & - & 0 & = & 20 \\
& & \dfrac{x}{4} & = & 20 \qquad \text{Multiply both sides by 4.} \\
4 \cdot & & \dfrac{x}{4} & = & 20 \cdot 4 \\
& & x & = & 80
\end{array}
$$

These are the steps for solving two-step equations.

1.  Add or subtract to get the variable and its coefficient on one side and a number on the other.
2.  Multiply or divide both sides to get rid of the coefficient.

Why do we do the steps in this order? Let's look at the following equation to see why:

$$3x + 5 = 14$$

If we divided by 3 first, we would end up with the following equation:

$$\frac{3x}{3} + \frac{5}{3} = \frac{14}{3}$$

Who wants to work with all those fractions, especially if we don't have to? So instead, let's subtract to simplify first. And then, we'll divide.

$$
\begin{array}{rcrcr}
3x & + & 5 & = & 14 \\
 & - & 5 & & -5 \\
\hline
3x & + & 0 & = & 9 \\
 & & \dfrac{3x}{3} & = & \dfrac{9}{3} \\
 & & x & = & 3 \\
\end{array}
$$

This is much easier. Getting rid of the coefficient will always be our last step.

ONE MORE THING... Math is often called the universal language. PEMDAS is a useful part of that language. In algebra, for example, we use the order of operations to solve for an unknown. Any time you use a formula, you are using the order of operations and algebra—and you will use formulas to solve for something in nearly any job. For instance, bankers, economists, and tourists use formulas to convert one type of currency into another. Variables such as $x$ are used in many ways in both math and other disciplines. A biologist may show, in a formula, how the number of rabbits in a forest varies with the number of foxes in the forest. If the biologist knows the number of foxes in the forest, she can use the formula to approximate the number of rabbits.

# Participate

## Activity: Hands-On

Try to write your own one-step algebra questions like $p - 2 = 10$ and challenge your partner or sibling to solve for the variable. Make sure you practice saying what inverse operation you are doing. For instance, for $p - 2 = 10$, addition is the inverse operation of subtraction, so add 2 to both sides. For something like $4x = 60$, division is the inverse operation of multiplication, so make sure you or your partner says "divide by 4 on both sides" as the step for this problem. Can you stump your partner with your equations?

# In a Nutshell

## Rules

- **PEMDAS:** Parentheses, Exponents, Multiplication & Division, Addition & Subtraction

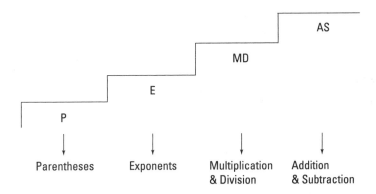

| | | | |
| --- | --- | --- | --- |
| Parentheses | Exponents | Multiplication & Division | Addition & Subtraction |

- Inverse operations are used to undo each other. Addition and subtraction are inverse operations. Multiplication and division are inverse operations.

- Any operation done to one side of an equation must also be done to the other side.

- To solve two-step equations, use the following steps:

  1. Add or subtract to get the variable and its coefficient on one side and a number on the other.

  2. Multiply or divide both sides to get rid of the coefficient.

**Answers for Dive Right In:**

1. $1

2. $2.80

3. $4.00

4. $16.80

5. 8 ounces

6. 112 ounces; 7 pounds

7. 160 ounces; 10 pounds

8. 61 ounces

9. Flat rate (or $13.00)

 **Answers for Explore: More PEMDAS:**

The steps for evaluating the expression are given below.

$= 6 \div 3 + 4 \times 3 + (6 \times 3) \div 9$

$= 6 \div 3 + 4 \times 3 + 18 \div 9$

$= 2 + 4 \times 3 + 18 \div 9$

$= 2 + 12 + 18 \div 9$

$= 2 + 12 + 2$

$= 14 + 2$

$= 16$

# Translating English into Math

**S**ometimes there are more words than numbers in a math problem. That's why they call them *word problems*. Sometimes you don't even see *any* numbers in a math problem. The problem with word problems is all the words!

At the end of this lesson, you will be able to:

- identify the code words and phrases in a word problem
- translate those words and phrases into math problems

**Parent's Corner**

Word problems can be overwhelming! Sixth graders often get lost staring at the giant paragraph and don't know where to start. Remember that a lot of word problems are bloated with totally unnecessary information. Always encourage your student to read and underline the *final* question in the word problem. That will give your child a way into the problem.

# Dive Right In!

## A Full Aquarium

**Directions:** Javier received an aquarium tank for his birthday and a $50 gift certificate to a local pet store. He would like to fill it with as many fish as possible, so he does research on compatible varieties. He learns that Siamese Fighting Fish are colorful and exotic-looking, but they fight with other fish. The Black Phantom Tetras are less colorful but enjoy schooling in groups of at least 3; however, they may fight any fish they outnumber. The Kissing Gouramis are happy in a community environment and are known for kissing plants and other fish. Sunrise Guppies are fun and diverse fish that live easily in a community of other fish and prefer a group of 5 or more of their own species. Siamese Fighting Fish cost $3.50 each, Black Phantom Tetras cost $1.99 each, Kissing Gouramis are $3.49 each, and Sunrise Guppies are $3.99 each.

Javier wants a tank with many different kinds of fishes. What is the largest number of fish that Javier can keep in one tank without any fighting?

*Answers can be found on page 267.*

# Explore

## Translating All Those Words

Let's practice translating with the word problem below about Tanya.

⇨ Tanya is figuring out how much time she needs to get ready for her date. She knows she'll need about 20 minutes to shower and then half that time to put her makeup on. It usually takes her 3 times as long to do her hair as it does to do her makeup, so she has to make time for that too. She has to decide what she's wearing, which usually takes half as long as it takes her to do her hair. How much time does Tanya need?

Sounds like she needs weeks, doesn't it? No, it's not that bad. When you see a big, wordy problem like this, you have to hunt for the information that you need.

1. What time is given to us directly? For which task do we know exactly how long Tanya takes?

2. Now, what do we do with this information? Everything can be figured out from here. We know it takes Tanya half as much time to do her makeup as it takes her to shower. How can we write that in math-speak?

3. Assign a variable to the time it takes Tanya to do her makeup. Let's use $m$. Translate "$m$ equals half the time it takes Tanya to shower" and solve for $m$.

4.  Now we know how much time it takes her to put her makeup on, *m*. What's the next piece of info that's related to the time it takes to do her makeup? It's hair, so assign a variable to the time it takes Tanya to do her hair. Let's use *h*. Translate "*h* equals 3 times *m*" and solve for *h*.

5.  We have one more task for Tanya. She has to choose her outfit. Let's call that *o*. Translate "*o* equals one half of *h*" and solve for *o*.

6.  Now we have all the separate times figured out. What's the total time Tanya needs?

With word problems, you should always start with what you know and figure out what you don't know using that information. We just did exactly that. We took a math problem with a bunch of words in it, assigned some variables to things we didn't know, and figured it all out.

*Answers can be found on page 267.*

# Not as Many Words, but You Still Need Translation

You might also see problems like this one.

1. What is one-half the product of 14 and 10?

It's still not so easy to see what needs to be done right away. Whenever you see *what* or *how much* or *what is the value*, it's a good idea to assign a *variable* to this, as we did with Tanya and her prep time. That means that instead of writing *what is* from the problem above, we pick a variable, *x,* and use that instead, setting it equal to the rest of the problem.

Here are some translations that will help you.

| ENGLISH-TO-MATH TRANSLATION TABLE | |
|---|---|
| **English** | **Math** |
| what, what is, what is the value, how much, how many | *x,* or any other variable |
| is, are, was, were, (any form of the verb *to be*), equals, makes | = |
| of, product, times | multiplication |
| quotient, divided by | division |
| sum, total, more than | addition |
| difference, less than | subtraction |
| percent | $\dfrac{x}{100}$ (you can use any variable) |

Now that we have these under our belts, let's go back to the original problem.

1. What is one-half the product of 14 and 10?

Translate each part from English to math.

    a. what is:

    b. one-half:

    c. the product of 14 and 10:

Write the whole equation here and solve.




2. What is 40% of half the difference between 284 and 178?

Translate each part from English to math.

    a. What is:

    b. 40%:

    c. of:

    d. half:

    e. the difference between 284 and 178:

Write the whole equation here and solve.

Remember, with word problems you find what you know and use that information to figure out everything else. Use the translation table to help turn a word problem into a math problem that's more manageable.

3.  Carmen is moving to a bigger apartment. The rent is 1.4 times as much as it was last year. If Carmen's rent is now $1,680, how much did she pay in rent last year?

    a.  What do we know?

    b.  What are we trying to figure out (what's unknown)?

    c.  Assign a variable to the unknown.

    d.  Translate the problem, using the variable and the translation table.

    e.  Solve for the variable.

4.  Jamie is renting a scooter for a 45-mile drive around the island. Gas costs $2.80 per gallon. If Jamie's scooter gets 30 miles per gallon, how much does Jamie spend on gas for his drive?

    a.  What do we know?

    b.  What are we trying to figure out?

    c.  Assign a variable to the unknown.

    d.  Translate the problem, using the variable and common sense.

    e.  Solve.

5. Jamie and Davis are renting scooters for a different 40-mile drive. Gas costs $2.50 per gallon. Jamie's scooter gets 30 miles per gallon. Davis spends 120% more on gas for the drive than Jamie does. How much does Davis spend on gas?

a. What do we know?

b. What are we trying to figure out?

c. Assign a variable to the unknown.

d. Translate the problem, using the variable and common sense.

e. Solve.

*Answers can be found on page 268.*

ONE MORE THING... You will see word problems throughout your school career and in your life outside of school. Figuring out how much paint you need to paint your bedroom or how much time it will take to drive to the beach involves math, but it's disguised in words. Anything you do that involves money is really a word problem in disguise. If you know how to see past the disguise and translate words into math, you will have no problem with word problems.

# Participate

## Activity: Hands-On

Imagine you and your sibling or partner are out to eat. Create a menu with different prices and select what you'd like to eat. Total up the bill of what you both ate. Add a sales tax of 10% to the total and then make sure to include a 20% tip on top of the post-tax amount. What is the grand total for the meal? If you split the bill 50/50, how much does each person pay?

# In a Nutshell

### Hints

- Focus on the code words in the word problem and ignore the unimportant words.

- Write out your equation piece by piece—each code word should have a place in the equation.

**Answers for Dive Right In:**

Siamese Fighting Fish are out because you can only have one in a tank without fighting. The greatest number of one species you can buy is the Tetras, at 25 fish, based on their price, but Javier wants lots of different fish. The most important rule will be that Guppies have to come in groups of at least 5. That's $3.99 × 5 = $19.95. This means that we can't have more than 5 Tetras, because they'll fight if they outnumber the Guppies. $1.99 × 5 = $9.95. We're up to about $30. More fish can be bought. If we add Gouramis, we need at least 5, so that there is no fighting. $3.49 × 5 = $17.45. Let's make sure we're spending less than $50. $19.95 + $9.95 + $17.45 = $47.35. That leaves us with $2.65. We could buy another Tetra, but that would cause fighting. Maybe a plant?

**Answers for Explore: Translating All Those Words:**

1. 20 minutes, a shower

2. $\frac{1}{2}(20)$

3. $m = 10$

4. $h = 3m$, so $h = 3(10)$. Therefore, $h = 30$.

5. If $o = \frac{1}{2}h$, and $o = \frac{1}{2}(30)$, then $o = 15$.

6. $20 + 10 + 30 + 15 = 75$ minutes or 1 hour and 15 minutes.

1. 70

   a. $x$

   b. $\dfrac{1}{2}$

   c. $14 \times 10$

2. $21\dfrac{1}{5}$ or 21.2

   a. $x$

   b. $\dfrac{40}{100}$

   c. $\times$

   d. $\dfrac{1}{2}$

   e. $(284 - 178)$

3. a. This year's rent ($1,680), and the magnitude of change (1.4)

   b. The actual amount of last year's rent

   c. $r$

   d. $1.4r = \$1,680$

   e. $r = \$1,200$

4. a. The distance driven (45 miles), cost per gallon ($2.80), scooter's miles per gallon (30)

   b. How much was spent on gas

   c. $g$

   d. $g = \$2.80\left(\dfrac{45}{30}\right) = \$2.80(1.5)$

   e. $g = \$4.20$

5. a. The distance driven (40 miles), cost per gallon ($2.50), J's scooter's miles per gallon, difference in what D paid (120% *more*).

   b. How much Davis spent on gas

   c. Davis = $d$; Jamie = $j$

   d. $j = \$2.50\left(\dfrac{40}{30}\right) = \$\dfrac{10}{3} \approx \$3.33; \ d = j + \left(\dfrac{120}{100} \times j\right)$

   e. $\approx \$7.33$

# Solving Inequalities

When you solve for a variable in an equation, you find the particular number that the variable is equal to. But variables do not always represent just one number. Sometimes variables represent a range of numbers that are less than or greater than some other number. So, **equations** are number sentences that tell that two or more numbers, terms, or expressions are equal. **Inequalities** are number sentences that tell that one number, term, or expression is less than or greater than another.

At the end of this lesson, you will be able to:

- recognize and write inequalities

- solve for a variable in an inequality

**Parent's Corner**

If your sixth grader is stressed out about inequalities, remind them that they already know how to solve inequalities because they already know how to solve *equations*. Make sure to memorize the only difference with inequalities: if we multiply or divide an inequality by a negative number, we must flip the inequality sign!

# Dive Right In!

## Creating Your Own

**Directions:** First, write three inequalities using any numbers, variables, and inequality sign. Then, solve each of the inequalities. Finally, identify which solution you found by changing the direction of the sign during one of the steps. Answers will vary.

1.  Inequality #1:

    a.  Solve:

    b.  Change the direction of the sign. Solve again:

2.  Inequality #2:

    a.  Solve:

    b.  Change the direction of the sign. Solve again:

3.  Inequality #3:

    a.  Solve:

    b.  Change the direction of the sign. Solve again:

4. Show a number added to a variable on one side of the first inequality.

5. Show a number subtracted from a variable on one side of the second inequality.

6. Show a variable subtracted from a number on one side of the third inequality.

# Explore

## Working with Inequalities

Let's begin with a simple number sentence. You already know that if the variable $x$ equals 10, you would write:

$$x = 10$$

If you need to show that another variable, $y$, is less than 10, you will need to use a symbol that means *less than*. For *less than*, we use the symbol <. So, we write the inequality this way:

$$y < 10$$

Now, suppose that you need to show that yet another variable, $n$, is greater than 10. You will need to use a symbol that means *greater than*. For *greater than*, we use the symbol >. So, we write the inequality this way:

$$n > 10$$

Notice that the open side of the *less than* and *greater than* signs faces the greater number or term.

Sometimes a variable might be less than *or* equal to a number. Or, a variable might be greater than *or* equal to a number. In these cases, a horizontal line is included just underneath the < or >. You can think of the horizontal line as part of the equal sign. This is how to write it:

$$p \leq 10$$

$$q \geq 10$$

There's nothing more to it than that. Just use <, >, $\leq$, or $\geq$ to show an inequality!

## Solving Inequalities: The Basics

Now that you can recognize and write inequalities, you know just about all you need to know to solve inequalities. That's because you isolate and solve for the variable in the same way you would for an equation with an equal sign.

Let's look at two very similar number sentences.

$2x + 4 = 10$                                        $2x + 4 < 10$

The steps to solve for $x$ in both number sentences are the same. Subtract 4 from both sides of each number sentence. Then divide both sides by 2.

| | |
|---|---|
| $2x + 4 = 10$<br>$\underline{-4 \quad -4}$<br>$2x + 0 = 6$<br>$\underline{2x} \quad = \underline{6}$<br>$2 \qquad 2$<br>$\quad x = 3$ | $2x + 4 < 10$<br>$\underline{-4 \quad -4}$<br>$2x + 0 < 6$<br>$\underline{2x} \quad < \underline{6}$<br>$2 \qquad 2$<br>$\quad x < 3$ |

So, in the equation, $x$ *equals* 3. In the inequality, $x$ is *less than* 3.

## Helpful Tips for Solving Inequalities

- Less than is expressed as <.
- Greater than is expressed as >.
- Less than or equal to is expressed as ≤.
- Greater than or equal to is expressed as ≥.
- When you are solving for a variable in an inequality, you can mostly treat the inequality sign just like an equal sign. However, if you multiply or divide both sides of an inequality by a negative number, the inequality sign changes direction.

## Solving Inequalities: There's a Twist

Although you can treat the inequality sign just like an equal sign when you solve for a variable, there is one special rule you must keep in mind. If you multiply or divide both sides of an inequality by a negative number, you need to "flip" the inequality sign. That is, you need to change a *less than* sign to a *greater than* sign, and a *greater than* sign to a *less than* sign.

Let's solve for $x$ in the inequality $10 - 2x > 16$ to see how it works.

| | |
|---|---|
| $10 - 2x > 16$ | |
| $10 - 2x > 16$ | Subtract 10 from both sides. Note that when you add or subtract negative numbers, the inequality sign does not change direction. |
| $\underline{-10 \qquad -10}$ | |
| $0 - 2x > 6$ | |
| $\dfrac{-2x}{-2} > \dfrac{6}{-2}$ | Divide both sides by $-2$. |
| $x < -3$ | Because we divided by a negative number, the inequality sign changes direction. |

So, $x$ is less than $-3$.

Why do we need to change the direction of the sign when we multiply or divide by a negative number? Suppose we are told that $2 < 10$. That is a true statement. Now, if we multiply both sides by $-1$, but don't change the direction of the sign, we end up with $-2 < -10$. But that statement is not true, because $-2$ is greater than $-10$. So, we must change the direction of the sign.

Now you can recognize, write, and solve inequalities!

 **ONE MORE THING...** Sometimes, we need to figure out the exact value of something, and sometimes we just need to know a range of values. For example, sometimes we need to know only that someone must be older than a certain age to see a movie, or that the newest smartphone is affordable to us only if it costs less than a certain amount.

# Participate

## Activity: Hands-On

Work with a sibling or partner to make a list of various fruits and vegetables. Create an inequality by comparing some foods you like less than others. For instance you might have: Celery < Broccoli. Try to create a multi-part inequality that describes your food preferences. If you really dislike onions, feel mixed about spinach, but love cauliflower, you could write: Onion < Spinach < Cauliflower. Share your inequality with your partner!

# In a Nutshell

## Definitions

- **Equation:** a number sentence that tells that two or more numbers, terms, or expressions are equal; $x = 5$ is an equation

- **Inequality:** a number sentence that tells that one number, term, or expression is less than or greater than another; $y > 3$ is an inequality

# Circles

Circle questions are very common on tests, but luckily they always come down to the same few rules.

Imagine that you are going to make a pizza. You have enough cheese to cover a square 12 inches by 12 inches. However, you want to make a round pizza that is 14 inches wide, plus another 2 inches for the crust. If you don't put cheese on the crust, do you have enough cheese to cover the pizza?

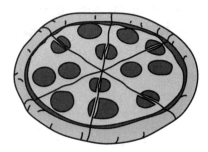

At the end of this lesson, you will be able to:

- identify the radius and diameter of a circle

- find and estimate the circumference of a circle

- find the area of a circle

---

**Parent's Corner**

Can you or your sixth grader draw a perfect circle *free hand*? Challenge each other to draw a circle and then have your student label the radius and diameter. Make sure your sixth grader has memorized the formula for circumference ($C = 2\pi r$ or $\pi d$) and area ($A = \pi r^2$) of a circle, as those formulas are important not only for sixth grade, but well beyond.

---

# Dive Right In!

## Running a Race

**Directions:** Racing tracks are often curved, but runners need to all run the same distance to the finish line to make the race fair. Study this information, and answer the questions.

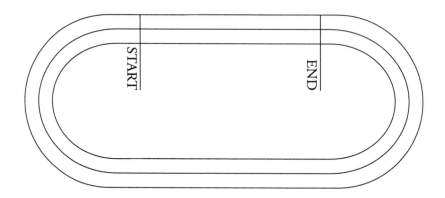

On the race track above, 2 runners are running a 100 m dash. The entire race is on a straight line, so both runners start at the same point, and both runners finish at the same point.

But what about a 200 m race? Now the racers are going to have to run around the curve before they get to the finish line. However, you may notice something unfair about this 200 m race.

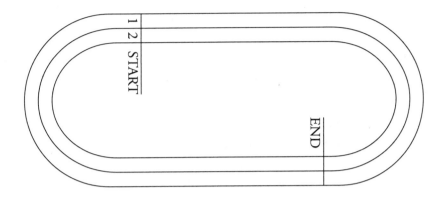

Notice that the person who starts at position 1 has a longer way to run around the curve than the person who starts at position 2. We're going to have to correct that to make sure that every runner runs exactly 200 m. First off, let's look at the measurements of the track. The curved lanes are each half of a circle.

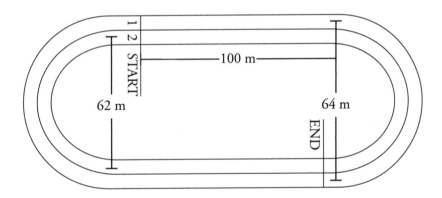

Use the previous information to answer these questions.

1.  What is the exact distance around the curve for the runner in position 1? What is the approximate distance?

2.  What is the exact distance around the curve for the runner in position 2? What is the approximate distance?

3.  If we want to make it a fair race, about how far back do we need to move the starting position for runner 2?

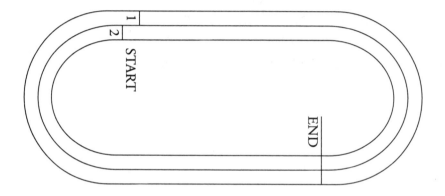

*Answers can be found on page 286.*

# Explore

## The Parts of a Circle

Before we work on circle problems, we're going to need to know the parts of a circle. First off, let's think about what makes a circle special: every single point on a circle is the same distance away from the center of the circle. This distance is called the **radius** of the circle. It is normally represented by an $r$.

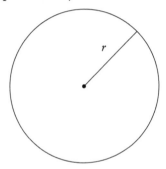

Any point from the center of the circle to the edge of the circle is always the same distance for any particular circle. So if we know the radius of a circle, we know *everything* we need to know for that circle. Every measurement for a circle can be calculated using the radius. So if you are ever stuck on a circle problem, try finding the radius.

It might sound funny, but two radiuses are called radii (RAY-dee-eye). If two radii meet, they form an angle in the center of the circle. This angle is called a **central angle**. In the following circle, the circle has a central angle of 60°.

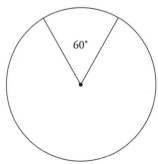

60°

The biggest possible central angle would go all the way around the circle. This angle is 360°.

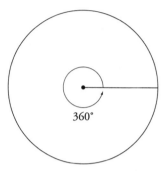

Let's say we drew a line from one point on the edge of the circle to some other point on the edge of the circle. That line is called a **chord**.

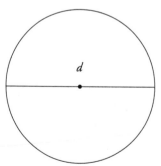

What's the longest chord possible? A line drawn from one edge of the circle to the other, passing through the center point. This chord is the **diameter** of the circle, and it is represented with a *d*.

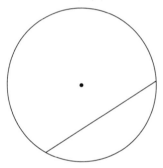

Because the diameter (*d*) goes through the center of the circle, it is the same as two radii (*r*). This is our first formula for circles:

$$d = 2r$$

# Circumference

The distance around the edge of a circle is known as its **circumference**. Circumference is represented by the letter $C$. How can we find the circumference of a circle? That's going to take a special number, $\pi$, which is spelled **pi** but pronounced "pie."

If you took a circle that was 1 meter wide (in other words, had a diameter of 1 m), cut it, and unrolled it, the unrolled circle would be

3.14159265358979323846264338327950288419716939937510582097494... meters long.

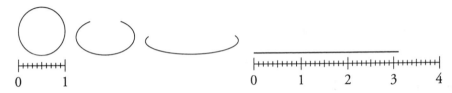

The digits of $\pi$ go way beyond what we've printed here. It's actually an **irrational number**, which means the digits never end and never repeat in a pattern. But we're not going to worry too much about that. Instead, rather than saying the circumference is 3.14159… meters long, we can just say that the circle has a circumference of $\pi$. If a circle is 2 meters wide (diameter is 2), then we can say that its circumference is $2\pi$, instead of 6.2831…and so on. This takes much less time to write!

Because $\pi$ is really close to 3, we have an excellent way of estimating the circumference of a circle: take the diameter and multiply it by 3.

A circle with $d = 4$ has a circumference of about 12.

A circle with $d = 1{,}000$ has a circumference of about 3,000.

A circle with $r = 5$ has a diameter of ($d = 2r$, so $d = 2 \times 5$) 10 and a circumference of about 30.

If we instead want an exact answer, we can use either of the two following formulas:

$$C = \pi d \qquad\qquad C = 2\pi r$$

A circle with $d = 3$ has a circumference of exactly $3\pi$.

A circle with $r = 100$ has a circumference of exactly ($2 \times 100 \times \pi$) $200\pi$.

# Area of a Circle

Now let's say we want to find the **area** ($A$), or space inside, a circle. To figure out the area, we're going to need the area formula:

$$A = \pi r^2$$

To find the area, we always need to know the radius. How would we find the area of a circle with a diameter of 10?

First off, we need to find the radius.

$$d = 2r$$

We know the diameter is 10, so we can plug that in for $d$.

$$10 = 2r$$

To solve for $r$, divide both sides by 2.

$$\frac{2r}{2} = \frac{10}{2}$$

$$r = 5$$

Now we can go back to our area formula. Always write out your formula without numbers as the first step.

$$A = \pi r^2$$

The radius is 5, so we can plug that into the equation.

$$A = \pi 5^2$$

Remember that if a value has a small raised number next to it, that small number is the **exponent**. In this formula, the little 2 means the number is **squared**. Squaring a number means to multiply it by itself. In our case, we have $5^2$, which is the same as $5 \times 5 = 25$.

$$A = 25\pi$$

That's our exact answer. We've left $\pi$ alone, so if someone wants to calculate the area of this circle to one million decimal places, they can do that by multiplying 25 times $\pi$, calculated out to a million decimal places. We probably don't need to spend all that time to get a good idea of what the answer will be. Instead, let's estimate about how big the area is. Because $\pi$ was approximately 3, we can estimate.

$$A \approx 25 \times 3$$

$$A \approx 75$$

# Participate

## Activity: Hands-On

Can you find a tree in your neighborhood? Take a tape measure and, with the help of a sibling or parent, measure all the way around the tree. What is the tree's circumference? Using that information and the formulas you've learned, can you figure out the radius of the tree? What about the area of its base?

# In a Nutshell

## Definitions

- A radius goes from the center of the circle to the edge.

- A central angle is the angle made by two radii in the center of the circle.

- There are 360° in a circle.

- A chord is any line that connects 2 points on a circle.

- A diameter is the longest chord.

## Formulas

- A diameter is the same as 2 radii.

$$d = 2r$$

- π (pi) is a number that is really close to 3. When possible, we'll just leave the symbol rather than multiply it out.

$$\pi \approx 3.14$$

- The circumference is the distance around the edge of a circle.

$$C = \pi d \qquad C = 2\pi r$$

- The area of a circle is everything inside the circle.

$$A = \pi r^2$$

 **Answers for Dive Right In:**

1. $32\pi \approx 96 \approx 100.48$ meters
2. $31\pi \approx 93 \approx 97.34$ meters
3. $\pi \approx 3 \approx 3.14$ meters. For comparison, this is about 10 feet.

# Triangles and Quadrilaterals

Imagine walking down the street. You come upon an intersection and you want to make a turn. What kind of turn could it be? Of course you could make a left or a right turn, but there are other ways to describe your turn. Some turns are very sharp, and some turns are more like slight bends. In math, we describe a turn by measuring the **angle**.

At the end of this lesson, you will be able to:

- tell the different types of angles

- name the different types of triangles and quadrilaterals

- find the perimeter and area of triangles and quadrilaterals

**Parent's Corner**

Triangles are a shape that sixth graders should get very comfortable with. Make sure they know the basic facts about triangles, including the formula for the area of a triangle [Area = $\frac{1}{2}$ (Base)(Height)], and the idea that there are 180 degrees in every triangle.

# Dive Right In!

## *Finding Geometry Everywhere*

**Directions:** Find the perimeter and area of household objects. Answers will vary.

1. Choose an angular object (such as a piece of paper) or a group of objects (such as 3 pencils or 3 toothbrushes or 4 books) in your home.

2. Put the object on your desk. If you have more than one, arrange the objects into a shape you can find the area of. Draw a picture of the figure you created.

3. Measure each side of your shape. Write the measurements on your figure.

4. What is the perimeter of your shape?

5. What is the area of your shape?

# Explore

## Types of Angles

There are several different types of angles. You can figure out the type of angle by looking at its size, measured in degrees.

**Acute** angles are angles smaller than 90°. In the figure below, you can see a 50° angle. Because 50° is smaller than 90°, this angle is an acute angle. What is the biggest an acute angle can be?

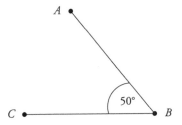

In this diagram, the two lines intersect at the corner point $B$. So we'll call point $B$ the vertex of the angle. A **vertex** is where two lines meet to create an angle. Now let's name the angle. We could simply call it "angle $B$" and write it as $\angle B$. However, this may not be clear enough. For example, in the diagram below, four different angles have point $B$ as a vertex. $\angle B$ could refer to any or all of these four angles!

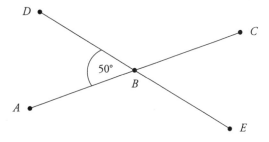

To be clearer, we'll name the angle after 3 points, putting the vertex in the middle. So we could call the angle $\angle ABD$ or $\angle DBA$. Using this method, name two other angles in the same diagram.

Another type of angle that we come across is a right angle. **Right** angles have measurements of exactly 90°. Looking at ∠*DEF* below, we see what a right angle looks like. Commonly, instead of writing 90°, we'll mark an angle as a right angle by putting a small square at the vertex. When you see this small square, you know that the two lines forming the angle are **perpendicular** to each other. When two perpendicular lines intersect, they create a right angle.

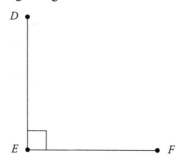

An angle that is greater than 90° is called an **obtuse** angle. ∠*XYZ* below is an obtuse angle because it is 150°.

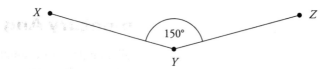

A straight line is also an angle, and is called a **straight angle**. Point *M* on line segment *LMO* below could also be called the vertex of ∠*LMO*. All straight lines are angles of exactly 180°.

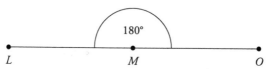

When you're working with angles, remember:
- Don't assume an angle is a right angle, even if it looks like one. You only know an angle is a right angle if you see the square in the vertex or if the angle is labeled as 90°.
- Acute angles are between 0° and 90°.
- Obtuse angles are between 90° and 180°.
- Only right angles are exactly 90°.
- Lines that make up a right angle are perpendicular to one another.
- Only straight angles (straight lines) are exactly 180°.

## Complementary and Supplementary Angles

Sometimes larger angles can be made up of two smaller angles. For example, in the figure below, $\angle ABC = 40°$ and $\angle CBD = 30°$. Add the two smaller angles together to find the size of the large angle: $\angle ABD = 70°$.

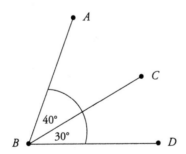

A special case occurs when the two smaller angles add up to either 90° or 180°. In the diagram below, ∠FGI is a right angle. This means that $x + y = 90°$.

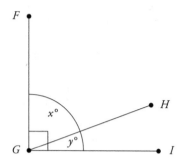

Because they add up to 90°, ∠FGH and ∠HGI are called **complementary angles**. If you were told that $x = 70$, how would you figure out the value of $y$? Because we know that $x + y = 90$ and $x = 70$, we get $y = 20$.

To solve for $y$, subtract 70 from both sides.

$70 + y = 90$

$y = 20$

If two angles combine to 180° make a straight angle, they are called **supplementary**. In the diagram below, the two angles are supplementary. Another way to say this is $x + y = 180$. If you are told that $y = 60$, then you are able to figure out that $x = 120$ the same way we did above.

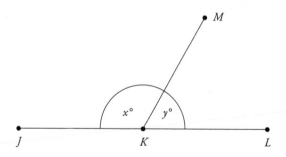

To solve for $x$, subtract 60 from both sides.

$60 + x = 180$

$x = 120$

# Triangles

A triangle is a geometry figure with three sides and three angles. Triangles can have all different shapes and sizes. Below you can see many of these types.

Even though there are many different types of triangles, there are certain things that are always true of all triangles.

 a. All triangles have exactly three sides.

 b. All triangles have exactly three angles.

 c. The angles within any triangle add up to 180°.

 d. The longest side is always opposite the largest angle.

 e. The shortest side is always opposite the smallest angle.

 f. Just as we did with angles, we can classify the different type of triangles. In fact, we can classify the different triangles by comparing the angles that make up the triangle.

# Obtuse, Right, and Acute Triangles

A triangle that has an obtuse angle is called an **obtuse triangle**. The two triangles below are examples of obtuse triangles.

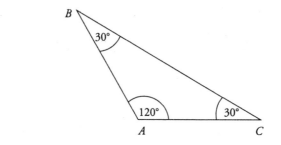

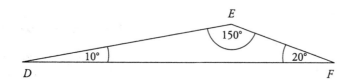

Any triangle that contains a right angle is a called a **right triangle**. The following triangle is a right triangle because $\angle C$ is a 90° angle.

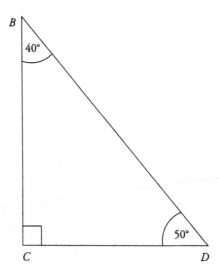

If a triangle is not a **right triangle** and not **obtuse,** it must be an **acute triangle.** In an **acute triangle**, all three angles are acute. Triangle *LMN* is acute because all the angles are smaller than 90°.

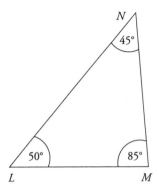

# Equilateral, Isosceles, and Scalene Triangles

Not only can we group triangles by the size of the angles, but also by how many equal angles (or equal sides) a triangle has. The first kind that we'll look at is the **equilateral triangle**.

An **equilateral triangle** is one in which all sides are equal and all angles are equal.

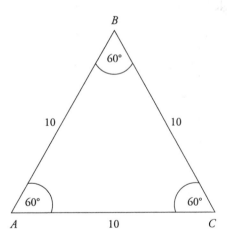

Remember, in any triangle, the interior angles have to add up to 180°. Therefore, in an equilateral triangle, each of the interior angles has to have a measure of exactly 60°. Because all the angles are less than 90°, any equilateral triangle must also be an acute triangle.

Triangles with at least two equal sides and two equal angles are called **isosceles triangles**. In an isosceles triangle, the two equal sides will always be opposite the two equal angles. Isosceles triangles can be acute, right, or obtuse. Each one of the below triangles is an isosceles triangle.

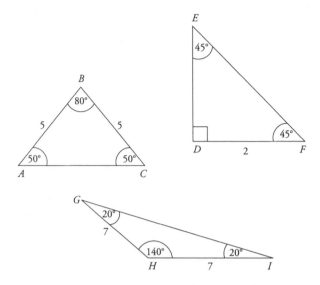

It's important to remember than an isosceles triangle has *at least* two equal angles and two equal sides. It may have three. So any equilateral triangle is also an isosceles triangle. An isosceles triangle may be acute, right, or obtuse, as seen is the previous diagrams. Can an equilateral triangle be an obtuse triangle?

Finally, any triangle in which all sides and all angles are different is called a **scalene triangle**. Scalene triangles can be acute, right, or obtuse. However, they *cannot* be equilateral or isosceles.

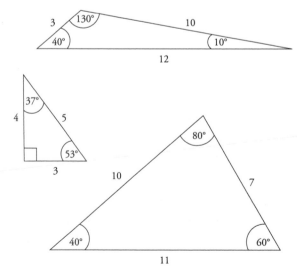

# Perimeter and Area of a Triangle

So far, we've been talking about measuring the individual parts of triangles. We've talked about measuring the lengths of the sides and the size of each angle. We can also measure the triangle as a whole. One way to measure the whole triangle is to measure the **perimeter**.

The **perimeter** of a triangle is the total distance around the triangle.

Imagine walking around a triangular track, going around one time, and finishing exactly where you started. How far did you walk? That distance is the perimeter. To find a triangle's perimeter, simply add the lengths of all three sides. Can you find the perimeter of each of the following triangles?

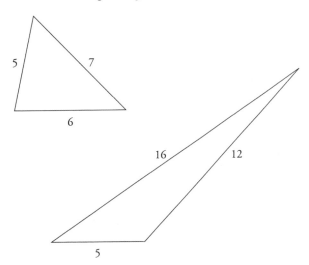

No matter what type of triangle you're looking at, you always find the perimeter the same way. You add the three sides together.

The **area**, however, may not always be as simple. The area is the size of a surface. Imagine your bedroom. Think about how much stuff you could fit into your room. The more stuff you can fit, the bigger the area of the room.

To figure out the area of a triangle you need to use this formula:

$$A = \frac{1}{2}bh$$

*A* represents the area, *b* represents the base, and *h* represents the height.

It's easiest to find the area of a right triangle. To find the area of a right triangle, you have to identify the **legs** of the triangle. The legs of a right triangle are the two sides that form the right angle. In the following triangle, the two legs are sides $\overline{AB}$ and $\overline{BC}$. Usually, we call the side on the bottom the base and the other leg the height. $\overline{AB} = 3$; this is our height ($h$). $\overline{BC} = 4$; this is our base ($b$).

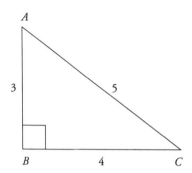

To find the area, we plug the base and the height into the formula.

$$A = \frac{1}{2}bh$$

$$A = \frac{1}{2}(4)(3)$$

$$A = 6$$

For other triangles, you may need more information than the sides of the triangle. For example, if we look at the triangle below, we see the sides are 10, 17, and 21.

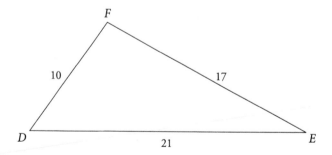

Since $\overline{DE}$ is on the bottom, we can say that the base is equal to 21.

But what is the height? Is it 10? Is it 17?

It's neither. The height always has to be perpendicular to the base. Neither $\overline{DE}$ or $\overline{EF}$ is. To figure out the height of this triangle, we need to draw an imaginary line from point

$F$ to the base $\overline{DE}$ to make a right angle at the base. The length of this line is the height. The figure below adds this imaginary line.

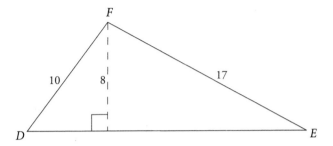

So we have a base of 21 and a height of 8. Let's plug those numbers into the formula for area of the triangle:

$$A = \frac{1}{2}bh$$

$$A = \frac{1}{2}(21)(8)$$

$$A = 84$$

Sometimes, for an obtuse triangle, the imaginary line forming the base falls outside the triangle. That's fine. Simply extend the base, as you see in the following diagram, and draw a line from the top vertex that is perpendicular to the extended base. This is the height.

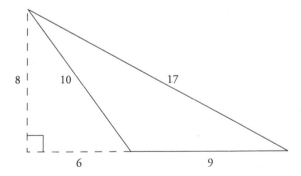

What is the area of the above triangle? Use the same formula as before.

$$A = \frac{1}{2}bh$$

$$A = \frac{1}{2}(9)(8)$$

$$A = 36$$

When you extend the base, don't count the length of the extra piece as your base. Only put the base of the original triangle is the formula. So, here, our base is 9 and not 15.

## Quadrilaterals

A **quadrilateral** is a geometric figure with exactly four sides. Just like triangles, there are many different types of quadrilaterals. The following things are true for all quadrilaterals.

    a.    All quadrilaterals have four sides and four angles.

    b.    The sum of the internal angles of all quadrilaterals is 360°.

    c.    The perimeter of a quadrilateral is equal to the sum of the four sides.

## Parallelograms

One common type of quadrilateral is a **parallelogram**. A parallelogram is a quadrilateral in which opposite sides are **parallel**. If two lines are parallel, this means that the lines *will never* intersect. The following lines are parallel.

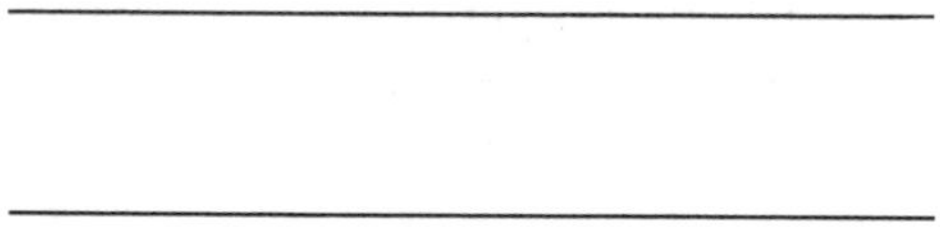

One example of a parallelogram is shown below. In any parallelogram, opposite sides are not only parallel, but also equal. Furthermore, opposite angles are equal, and angles next to each other, or adjacent, are supplementary. To find the area of a parallelogram, you use the formula $A = bh$.

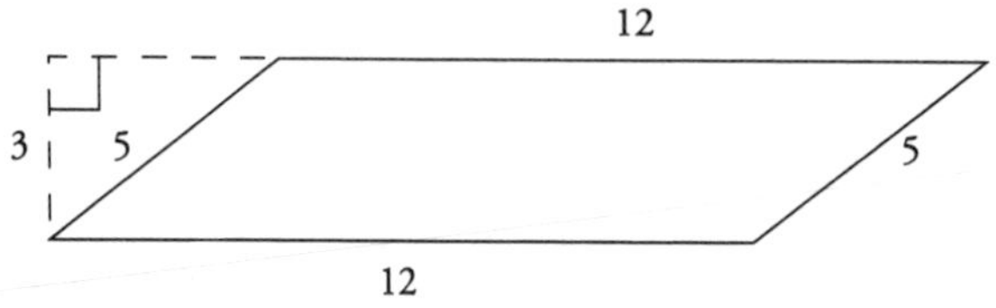

Just as in a triangle, the height of a parallelogram must be perpendicular to the base. What would be the area of the above parallelogram?

$$A = bh$$

$$A = (12)(3)$$

$$A = 36$$

## Rectangles

Another common type of quadrilateral is a **rectangle**. A rectangle is a parallelogram in which all angles are exactly 90°. To find the area of a rectangle, we can use the same formula we use for any parallelogram. However, because the angles are all 90°, one of the sides of the rectangle can be used as its height. Therefore, we write the area formula for rectangles as $A = lw$. This stands for *area* equals *length* times *width*. Let's look at the rectangle, below.

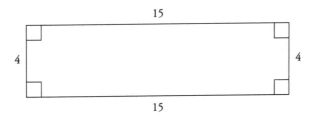

The length of the rectangle is 15 and the height, or width, is 4. Plug those numbers into the formula for area:

$$A = lw$$

$$A = (15)(4)$$

$$A = 60$$

# Squares

A **square** is a parallelogram that is a rectangle with equal sides. Therefore, a square has all of the following properties:

    a.    Opposite sides are parallel.
    b.    All four sides are equal.
    c.    All four angles are 90°.
    d.    The diagonals are perpendicular.

Because a square is a parallelogram, we can use the area formula $A = bh$. Because a square is also a rectangle, we can use $A = lw$. However, because the length and width are equal in a square, it is more common to use $A = s^2$.

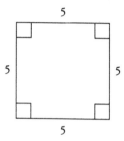

Looking at the square above, because the side is 5, we find the area by doing:

$$A = s^2$$

$$A = 5^2$$

$$A = 25$$

# Trapezoids

Another type of quadrilateral is a **trapezoid**. A trapezoid is quadrilateral that has exactly one pair of parallel sides. Because there's only one pair of parallel sides, a trapezoid cannot be a parallelogram, a rectangle, or a square. The figure below is a trapezoid.

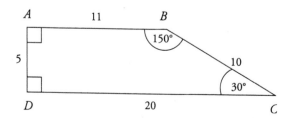

Some trapezoids are **isosceles trapezoids**. An isosceles trapezoid is a trapezoid in which the two non-parallel sides are equal. Here is an example.

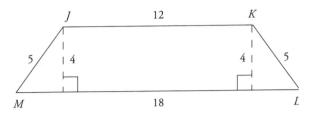

Because trapezoids are not parallelograms, we need a different formula to find their area. Instead of $A = bh$ or $A = lw$, we'll use $A = h\left(\dfrac{b_1 + b_2}{2}\right)$. In this equation, $b_1$ and $b_2$ represent the lengths of the two parallel sides, and $h$ represents the height of the trapezoid. Once again, the height has to be perpendicular to the base. To figure out the area of the above trapezoid, we follow these steps:

$$A = h\left(\frac{b_1 + b_2}{2}\right)$$

$$A = 4\left(\frac{12 + 18}{2}\right)$$

$$A = 60$$

 **ONE MORE THING...** Understanding perimeters and conversions can help you understand sports. Suppose you wanted to know which involved more running, the 100-yard dash or an inside-the-park home run. If you know that a baseball diamond is a square in which each side is 90 feet, you can find out that it has a perimeter of 360 feet. If you know that there are 3 feet in a yard, you can figure out that the 100 yard dash involves running 300 feet. Therefore, running around a baseball diamond once involves more running than the 100-yard dash.

# Participate

## Activity: Hands-On

Make a "Shape Collage." Cut different shapes from construction paper (make sure at least one is a triangle!) Write the name of the shape on a separate piece of paper. Then, glue the shapes to a large sheet of construction paper to make a collage. Decorate your collage as you wish. Then, measure the sides of all your shapes. What is the total perimeter of your collage? Can you calculate the total area of your collage?

# In a Nutshell

## Definitions

- **Acute angles:** angles that are smaller than 90°

- **Right angles:** angles that are exactly 90°

- **Obtuse angles:** angles that are bigger than 90°

- **Complementary angles:** a pair of angles with a sum of 90°

- **Supplementary angles:** a pair of angles with a sum of 180°

- **Acute triangles:** triangles in which every angle is acute

- **Right triangles:** triangles having one right angle

- **Obtuse triangles:** triangles that have one obtuse angle

- **Parallelogram:** a quadrilateral in which opposite sides are parallel

- **Rectangle:** a parallelogram in which all angles are right angles

- **Square:** a parallelogram that is both a rectangle and a rhombus

- **Trapezoid:** a quadrilateral with exactly one pair of parallel sides

- **Perimeter:** the distance around a shape

- **Area:** the space inside a shape

- **Base:** the bottom side of a shape

- **Height:** the distance from the base to the top of a shape. The height has to be perpendicular to the base.

# In a Nutshell (it's a big nutshell!)

**Rules**

- The sum of the interior angles of a triangle is 180°.

- The sum of the interior angles of a quadrilateral is 360°.

- Area of a triangle = $\frac{1}{2}bh$

- Area of a parallelogram = $bh$

- Area of a rectangle = $lw$

- Area of a square = $s^2$

- Area of a trapezoid = $h\left(\dfrac{b_1+b_2}{2}\right)$

# The Coordinate Plane

**M**aps show where places are. Maps also show where places are in relation to other places. So you can use a map to help you get from where you are to where you'd like to be. You can also use a map to figure out the distances between places. The **coordinate plane** is like a map.

At the end of this lesson, you will be able to:

- name parts of the coordinate plane

- find, plot, and name points on the coordinate plane

- find the perimeter and area of rectangles and polygons that are composites of rectangles on the coordinate plane

**Parent's Corner**

The coordinate plane is a fun way to create images and designs using math. Beyond doing math problems, encourage your sixth grader to play around with graph paper and plotting points on the coordinate plane. What shapes do you see when you connect the dots? Check that your student understands the location of the four quadrants and how negative and positive $x$ and $y$ values define the quadrants.

# Dive Right In!

## *Founders' Hill Park*

**Directions:** Complete the map of Founders' Hill Park, as shown below.

Founders' Hill Monument is at the origin. Plot the point, and label it.

There is a dog run at Founders' Hill Park. The corners of the dog run are at (10, 20), (20, 20), (20, 5), and (10, 5). Plot these points and draw lines connecting them. Label the resulting rectangle "Dog Run."

There is an iron fence around Founders' Hill. The corners of the fence are at (−15, 20), (10, 20), (10, −5), and (−15, −5). Plot these points, and draw lines connecting them. Label the resulting rectangle "Founders' Hill."

## FOUNDERS' HILL PARK

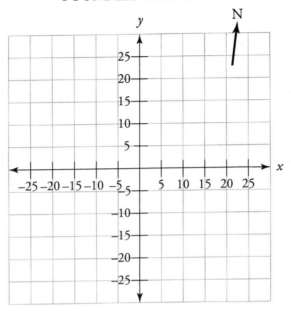

Use the map to answer some questions about Founders' Hill Park. Each unit on the map represents 1 meter.

1. What is the perimeter of Founders' Hill?

2. What is the area of Founders' Hill?

3. What is the perimeter of Founders' Hill Park, including both Founders' Hill and the dog run?

4. What is the area of Founders' Hill Park, including both Founders' Hill and the dog run?

*Answers can be found on page 322.*

# Explore

## Inside the Coordinate Plane

First, let's learn some terms we'll need to understand in order to use this map. Look at the coordinate plane. It is really a two-dimensional number line.

The **x-axis** on the coordinate plane is like the number line you are probably already familiar with. It is horizontal. It goes right and left. Numbers increase in value, or get bigger, as they go right on the x-axis. They decrease in value as they go left on the x-axis.

The **y-axis** on the coordinate plane is a vertical number line. It goes up and down. Numbers increase in value as they go up the y-axis. They decrease in value as they go down the y-axis.

The x-axis and y-axis meet at 0 on both number lines. This point is called the **origin**. The x-axis and y-axis also divide the coordinate plane into four parts. Each part is called a **quadrant**.

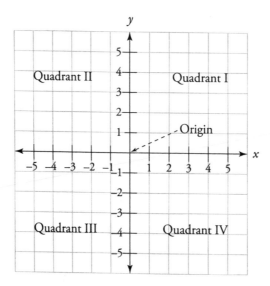

Numbers to the right of the origin on the x-axis are positive, and numbers to the left of the origin on the x-axis are negative. Numbers above the origin on the y-axis are positive, and numbers below the origin on the y-axis are negative.

| Quadrant | Value of $x$ | Value of $y$ |
| --- | --- | --- |
| Quadrant I | positive | positive |
| Quadrant II | negative | positive |
| Quadrant III | negative | negative |
| Quadrant IV | positive | negative |

## Finding and Plotting Points on the Coordinate Plane

Specific locations, or **points**, on the coordinate plane are each given an **ordered pair**, like this one:

$$(4, 2)$$

Each number in an ordered pair is called a **coordinate**. The first coordinate is called the $x$-coordinate and tells the value of $x$. It tells how many steps, or units, to go right or left from the $y$-axis. The second coordinate is called the $y$-coordinate and tells the value of $y$. It tells how many units to go up or down from the $x$-axis.

Let's find (4, 2) on the coordinate plane. The $x$-coordinate is positive, so we know to go right from the $y$-axis. Start at the origin, and go 4 units right.

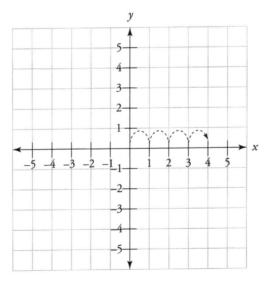

The *y*-coordinate is also positive, so we know to go up from the *x*-axis. Go 2 units up.

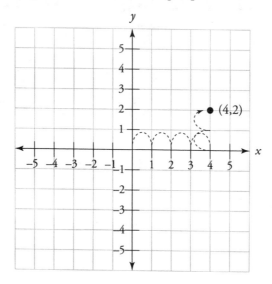

This process is the best way to find and plot a point on the coordinate plane. Start at the origin, then move right or left along the *x*-axis to the value given by the *x*-coordinate. Then move the number of units and in the direction given by the *y*-coordinate. Go up if the value is positive and down if the value is negative.

## Naming a Point on the Coordinate Plane

The coordinate plane below shows a map of a carnival. A carousel is at the origin. What ordered pair tells where the entrance to the fun house is?

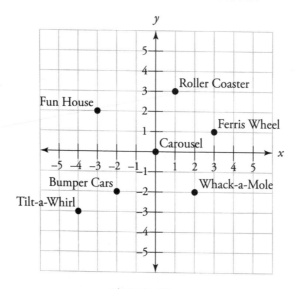

The entrance to the fun house is 3 units to the left of the y-axis and 2 units up from the x-axis. It is in Quadrant II. Remember, in Quadrant II, values of x are negative and values of y are positive. So the value of x is −3, and the value of y is 2. The ordered pair is (−3, 2).

Notice how the point showing the entrance to the fun house lines up with the −3 labeled on the x-axis and the 2 labeled on the y-axis.

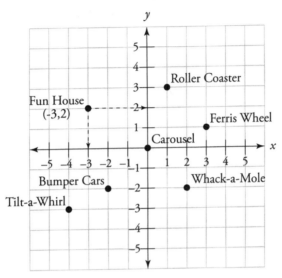

## Finding the Perimeter of Polygons

A **polygon** is a closed figure made by joining lines, such as rectangles, trapezoids, and octagons. We can find the perimeter and area of polygons and other figures that are mapped on the coordinate plane. First, let's review perimeter and area.

The **perimeter** of a figure is the distance around the figure. To find the perimeter of a polygon, add the lengths of the sides of the polygon.

The lengths of the sides of this rectangle are labeled. Remember, the opposite sides of a rectangle are equal in length.

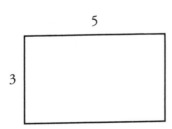

Perimeter = 5 + 3 + 5 + 3                     Add the lengths of the sides.

Perimeter = 16 units                          Remember to label your answer.

You can find the perimeter of an irregular polygon in the same way you find the perimeter of a rectangle. Just add the lengths of the sides.

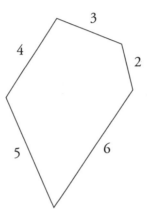

$P = 4 + 3 + 2 + 6 + 5$                        Add the lengths of the sides.

$P = 20$ units                                 Remember to label your answer.

## Finding the Area of Rectangles

The **area** of a figure is the amount of space covered by the figure. For example, let's say you were planning to cover a floor with tiles. You would find the area of the floor in order to find out how many tiles you need to cover the floor.

Let's say that you plan to use square tiles with sides 1 foot long. And let's say that the floor you plan to cover with these tiles is 10 feet long and 8 feet wide.

10 feet

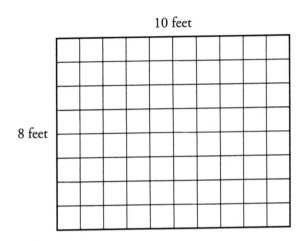

8 feet

To find the area of the floor, you could count the number of square units shown in the diagram. Or you could multiply the length and the width of the rectangle in the diagram.

$A = l \times w$    Area is the length times the width of the rectangle.

$A = 10 \times 8$    Plug the values into the formula.

$A = 80$ square feet    Remember to label your answer.

You would need 80 tiles to cover this floor.

What if the floor you plan to cover is an irregular shape, like the one shown below?

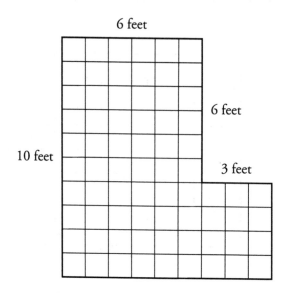

Again, to find the area of the floor, you could count the number of square feet shown in the diagram. Or you might notice that this irregular shape is made of two rectangles.

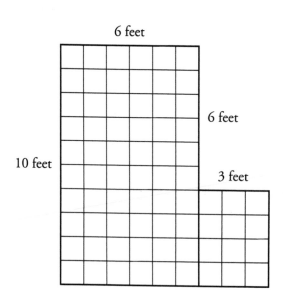

First, subtract to find the width of the smaller rectangle: 10 – 6 = 4. Now you can use the formula to find the area of each rectangle. Then, add the two areas.

$A = (l \times w) + (l \times w)$        The area of the floor is the area of the two rectangles added together.

$A = (6 \times 10) + (3 \times 4)$        Plug the values into the formula.

$A = 60 + 12$        Add the areas of the two rectangles.

$A = 72$ square feet        Remember to label your answer.

You would need 72 tiles to cover this floor.

# Finding Perimeter and Area on the Coordinate Plane

The coordinate plane below shows a rectangle. Ordered pairs give the coordinates for each **vertex**, or corner, of the rectangle. How can we use the coordinate plane to find the perimeter and area of the rectangle?

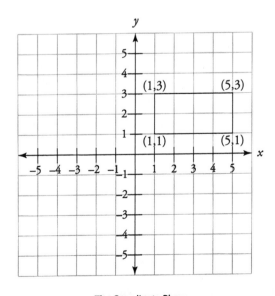

First, we need to find the length and width of the rectangle. Once we know the length and width of the rectangle, we can add to find the perimeter and multiply to find the area.

Let's find the length of the rectangle by finding the distance between (5, 1) and (1, 1). The horizontal distance between two points is the **absolute value** of the difference between their $x$-coordinates. Remember, absolute value just makes the number or answer positive. The $x$-coordinates of (5, 1) and (1, 1) are 5 and 1. $|5 - 1| = 4$, so the rectangle is 4 units long. You can check by counting the number of units between (5, 1) and (1, 1).

Similarly, we can find the width of the rectangle by finding the distance between (1, 3) and (1, 1). The vertical distance between two points is the absolute value of the difference between their $y$-coordinates. The $y$-coordinates of (1, 3) and (1, 1) are 3 and 1. $|3 - 1| = 2$, so the rectangle is 2 units wide. You can check by counting the number of units between (1, 3) and (1, 1).

Now that we know the length and width of this rectangle, we can find the perimeter and area. Remember, the opposite sides of a rectangle are equal in length.

First, we add to find the perimeter.

$P = 4 + 2 + 4 + 2$        Add the lengths of the sides.

$P = 12$ units        Remember to label your answer.

Next, we multiply to find the area.

$A = l \times w$        Area is the length times the width of the rectangle.

$A = 4 \times 2$        Plug the values into the formula.

$A = 8$ square units        Remember to label your answer.

**ONE MORE THING...** The coordinate plane shows up in both geometry and algebra classes because it offers a way to analyze geometric figures algebraically. The coordinate plane is also used to show functional relationships, or, in other words, how values of $y$ relate to values of $x$. You can add another axis to the coordinate plane to create a three-dimensional coordinate grid. Three-dimensional grids are used to create the computer-generated images you see in video games and movies.

# Participate

## Activity: Hands-On

Using graph paper, try to map your neighborhood on the coordinate plane. Make the *y*-axis the North-South directions and the *x*-axis the East-West directions. Plot points for locations such as your home, your friend's home, your school, your favorite store, etc. What are the (*x,y*) coordinate points for those locations?

# In a Nutshell

**Definitions**

- **Coordinate plane**: a two-dimensional number line

- **x-axis**: the horizontal number line on the coordinate plane; $y = 0$ at the x-axis

- **y-axis**: the vertical number line on the coordinate plane; $x = 0$ at the y-axis

- **Origin**: the point on the coordinate plane where the x-axis and y-axis intersect; both x and y equal 0 at the origin

- **Quadrant**: one of the four parts into which the x-axis and y-axis divide the coordinate plane

- **Point**: a specific location on the coordinate plane

- **Ordered pair**: a pair of numbers that tells the location of a point on the coordinate plane; for example, (5, 2)

- **Coordinate**: one of the pair of numbers in an ordered pair; the first coordinate tells the value of x, and the second coordinate tells the value of y

- **Perimeter**: the distance around a figure

- **Area**: the amount of space covered by a figure

**Rules**

- The horizontal distance between two points is the absolute value of the difference between their x-coordinates.

- The vertical distance between two points is the absolute value of the difference between their y-coordinates.

FOUNDERS' HILL PARK

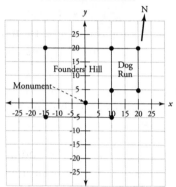

1. 100 meters

2. 625 square meters

3. 110 meters

4. 775 square meters

# Three-Dimensional Objects

**Y**ou will need to solve math problems involving three-dimensional objects throughout your life, as well as on various test types. Imagine you want to decorate a box to give to a friend as a birthday present. You have colorful stickers that you want to use to cover the box. Each sticker covers 1 square inch of the box. How many stickers will you need? The dimensions of the box are shown in the following diagram.

To find the number of stickers that will cover the box, you need to find the **surface area.** The surface area of a three-dimensional figure is the sum of the areas of the sides. The box has six sides. We can calculate the area of each rectangular side using the formula for the area of a rectangle, $l \times w$. Or, better yet, we can use a special formula for the surface area.

At the end of this lesson, you will be able to:

- find the surface area of a three-dimensional object

- find the volume of a three-dimensional object

- identify the elements of a three-dimensional object

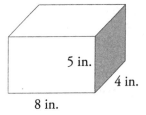

5 in.

4 in.

8 in.

---

**Parent's Corner**

Moving from 2-dimensional objects like circles and triangles to 3-dimensional objects like rectangular prisms can be a challenging leap for sixth graders. Try not to merely memorize formulas for the volumes of figures, but, rather, help your student understand the way area and volume are related. For instance, sixth graders will know that to calculate the area of a rectangle, we multiply length by width. To find the area of a rectangular prism, simply add height to that calculation: length × width × height. Voilà! We've added another *dimension*.

# Dive Right In!

## *Making Your Own Three-Dimensional Figures*

**Directions:** Create your own three-dimensional figure. Then estimate and solve for its surface area and volume. Answers will vary.

Come up with a three-dimensional figure to work with. Choose a cube or type of prism, because they are easier to work with. Decide a different dimension of the figure, such as the length, height, and width.

Use the information from your figure work to answer these questions.

1. How many faces does your figure have? _____

2. How many edges does your figure have? _____

3. How many vertices does your figure have? _____

4. What is the length of your figure? _____

5. What is the width of your figure? _____

6. What is the height of your figure? _____

Do you remember the formulas for the surface area and volume for your three-dimensional figure? Write them below. Take a look at the formulas throughout this chapter if you need to.

7.     What is the formula for the surface area of your figure?

8.     What is the formula for the volume of your figure?

Take a good look at your figure. Without doing any calculations, take a guess: estimate the surface area and volume of your figure.

9.     What is your estimate for the surface area of your figure?
       _____

10.    What is your estimate for the volume of your figure? _____

Now, use the formulas for the surface area and volume for your three-dimensional figure. Plug in your values, and write the final values on the lines below. Don't forget that surface area is given in square units, and volume is given in cubic units.

11.    What is the surface area of your figure? _____

12.    What is the volume of your figure? _____

13.    Compare your estimates to the actual surface area and volume. How close were you?

# Explore

## Surface Area Formulas for Common Solid Figures

These are the surface area formulas for common three-dimensional objects:

- Cube: $6a^2$, where $a$ is the length of one side
- Rectangular prism: $2lw + 2lh + 2wh$, where $l$ is the length, $w$ is the width, and $h$ is the height
- Prism: $2b + Ph$, where $b$ is the area of the base, $P$ is the perimeter of the base, and $h$ is the height
- Cylinder: $2\pi r^2 + 2\pi rh$, where $r$ is the radius of the cylinder and $h$ is its height

## Using a Formula for Surface Area

Because the box in the previous question is a rectangular prism, we'll use the formula $2lw + 2lh + 2wh$. What do the variables stand for? Well, the length is 8 inches, the width is 4 inches, and the height is 5 inches. Let's plug those numbers in and simplify!

$$2lw + 2lh + 2wh$$

$$2(8 \text{ in.})(4 \text{ in.}) + 2(8 \text{ in.})(5 \text{ in.}) + 2(4 \text{ in.})(5 \text{ in.})$$

$$2(32 \text{ sq. in.}) + 2(40 \text{ sq. in.}) + 2(20 \text{ sq. in.})$$

$$64 \text{ sq. in.} + 80 \text{ sq. in.} + 40 \text{ sq. in.}$$

$$184 \text{ sq. in.}$$

The surface area of the box is 184 square inches. To cover it with colorful 1-square-inch stickers, you would need 184 of the stickers.

# Finding Volume

Sometimes you need to find the volume of a three-dimensional object. For example, let's say you buy a bag of rice and want to put it in an airtight plastic bin for long-term storage. The bag says it holds 150 cubic inches of rice. The dimensions of the plastic bin are shown below. You need to know how much space is inside the plastic bin before you empty the rice into it.

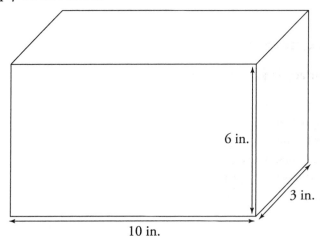

Once again, we'll want to use a formula. This time we'll need to use a formula for volume, which is the amount of space inside a three-dimensional figure.

## Volume Formulas for Common Solid Figures

These are the surface area formulas for common three-dimensional objects:

- Cube: $a^3$, where $a$ is the length of one side
- Rectangular prism: $lwh$, where $l$ is the length, $w$ is the width, and $h$ is the height
- Prism: $Bh$, where $B$ is the area of the base and $h$ is the height
- Cylinder: $\pi r^2 h$, where $r$ is the radius of the cylinder and $h$ is its height

## Using a Formula for Volume

Because the box in the question is a rectangular prism, we'll use the formula $lwh$. That just means we have to multiply the lengths of the three dimensions, and the product is the volume.

Let's plug those numbers in and simplify!

$$lwh$$

$$(10 \text{ in.})(3 \text{ in.})(6 \text{ in.})$$

$$180 \text{ in.}^3$$

The volume of the box is 180 cubic inches. You would have plenty of room for the rice in the bag to fit in the plastic bin. In fact, you'd have 30 cubic inches to spare!

## Elements of Three-Dimensional Objects

You may need to find an element of a three-dimensional object, such as the number of faces, corners, or edges. A face is a two-dimensional surface of a three-dimensional figure. An edge is a line that is formed when two faces are connected. A corner, or a **vertex**, is the point on a three-dimensional figure when three faces are connected. In the figure below, there are 6 faces, 12 edges, and 8 vertices. (The plural of vertex is vertices.)

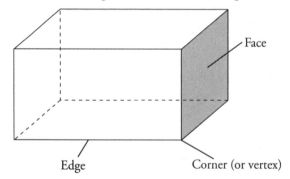

Edge      Corner (or vertex)

**ONE MORE THING...** Everything you touch in your real life is three-dimensional. So it's fair to say that working with and understanding three-dimensional objects is something that you'll use often, and that it's pretty important. Plus, if you ever work in any type of building or construction—carpentry, architecture, or even painting—you will use these formulas all the time.

# Participate

## Activity: Hands-On

Look around your room: can you find one object that is a cube and one that is a rectangular prism? Using the formulas you learned, calculate the surface area and volume of both objects! Keep going! How many cubes and rectangular prisms can you find?

# In a Nutshell

**Rules**

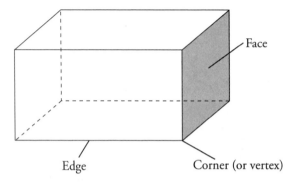

Face

Edge          Corner (or vertex)

- When you need to find the surface area of a three-dimensional figure, you need to find the sum of all the sides. Alternatively, you can use a formula for the shape.

- When you need to find the volume of a three-dimensional figure, you need to find the amount of space inside if it. You can use the formula, $V = lwh$, for a rectangular prism.

# NOTES